Mediterranean Diet on a Budget

MEDITERRANEAN
DIET on a Budget

Recipes, Meal Plans, and Tips to Eat Healthfully for as Little as $50 a Week

Emily Cooper, RD

**ROCKRIDGE
PRESS**

Interior and Cover Designer: Stephanie Mautone
Art Producer: Melissa Malinowksy
Editor: Owen Holmes
Production Editor: Caroline Flanagan
Production Manager: Martin Worthington

Photography © Alicia Cho, Hélène Dujardin, cover and p. ii; Darren Muir, pp. viii, 11, 48, 99; Marija Vidal, pp. x, 24; Hélène Dujardin, pp. 20, 28, 34, 40, 59; Thomas J. Story, pp.16, 28, 37, 75, 80, 130, 142; Annie Martin, pp. 20, 24; 51, 62, 65, 66, 83, 96, 116, 119, 133; Nadine Greeff/Stocksy, p. 90; Ivan Solis, p. 105; Evi Abeler, p. 120; All illustrations used under license from Shutterstock.

Paperback ISBN: 978-1-63878-363-3
eBook ISBN: 978-1-63878-523-1
R0

Dedicated to my biggest cheerleaders. You know who you are. I'm forever grateful.

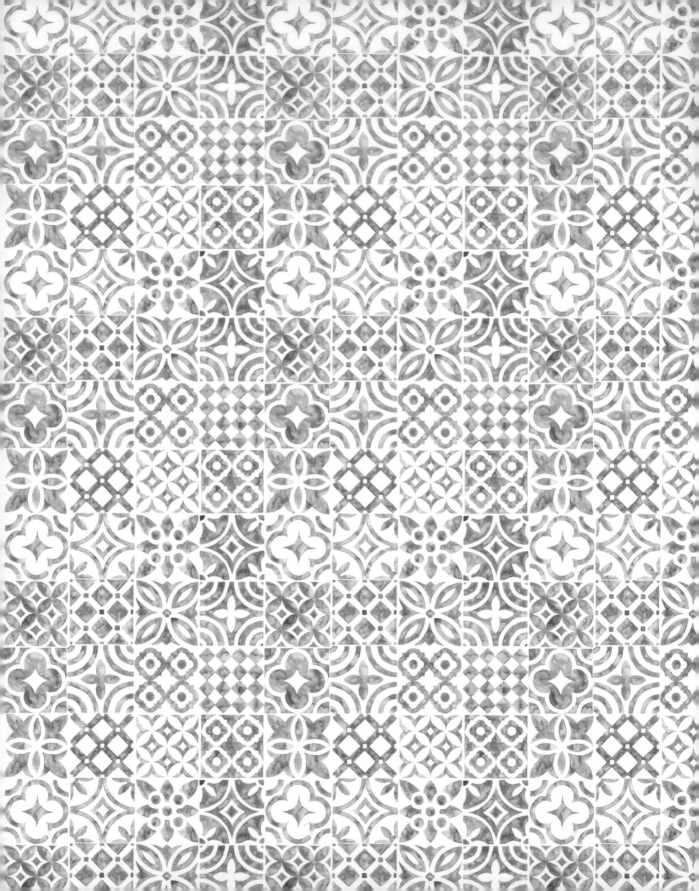

CONTENTS

INTRODUCTION

WELCOME TO *MEDITERRANEAN DIET ON A BUDGET*!

As a registered dietitian nutritionist, I know the struggles many people face when adopting a healthier way of eating: Some recipes call for expensive ingredients, take too much time, or require special techniques. Not to mention many healthy foods have picked up the reputation of tasting boring. But the Mediterranean diet has held the top spot for best overall diet four years in a row for a good reason. Because it is more of an eating pattern than a prescribed "diet," it is easy to follow; includes a balance of protein, carbohydrates, and healthy fats; and can be helpful with heart and brain health, weight maintenance, and diabetes. I'm here to show you that embracing healthier eating habits by adopting a Mediterranean diet doesn't have to be difficult, expensive, or bland.

Everyone comes to the Mediterranean diet for a different reason. It could be to reach specific health goals, maintain a healthier lifestyle, or simply incorporate more nutrient-rich and flavorful foods and recipes into your weekly routine. Whatever your reason, you've come to the right place.

Getting into the groove of any new eating pattern can take some effort. That's why this cookbook is designed so you can follow the Mediterranean diet principles using easy recipes and affordable ingredients that don't sacrifice flavor or nutrition. Whether you are just getting started or already familiar with the Mediterranean diet, I'm confident you will find the recipes, meal plans, and money-saving tips in this book easy and completely doable, no matter how busy the week gets.

I hope that *Mediterranean Diet on a Budget* helps you achieve and maintain your lifestyle goals while enjoying inexpensive and nourishing Mediterranean-inspired foods along the way.

Let's get started!

AN AFFORDABLE APPROACH TO THE MEDITERRANEAN DIET

In this chapter, I'll go over the basics of the Mediterranean diet and show you how to stick to your budget and even save money while adopting this new way of cooking and eating.

Fresh, Healthy Food That
Won't Break the Bank

The Mediterranean diet is not a diet in the conventional sense. It's more of a road map for a way of eating that incorporates nutrient-rich foods more often while still including your favorite foods in moderation. It emphasizes fruits, vegetables, lean proteins, whole grains, and healthy sources of fats, with room for the occasional treat. It is influenced and inspired by the dishes, ingredients, and eating patterns found in the countries that border the Mediterranean Sea, including Spain, France, Italy, Greece, Israel, Morocco, Libya, Lebanon, Algeria, Tunisia, and Egypt.

Although the exact origins of the Mediterranean diet are still up for debate, it has been around for centuries. Its ever-growing popularity over the past few decades is attributed to the range of health benefits it provides and its simplicity, emphasis on bold flavors, and the ease of adopting it into everyday life.

Some common misconceptions around the Mediterranean diet are that it is costly, the dishes are difficult to prepare, and it comes with a long list of hard-to-find ingredients. Despite what you may have heard, following the Mediterranean diet does not require spending your entire paycheck on expensive meats, seafood, or other grocery items. Nor does it require hunting down a laundry list of specialty ingredients at multiple grocery stores or dedicating an entire day to being in the kitchen. Some of the traditional, healthy dishes unique to the Mediterranean region *can* involve more time, cooking experience, or unique ingredients—and they are worth the extra effort—but preparing these types of meals is not necessary to enjoy the flavors and health benefits that a Mediterranean-style diet can provide.

In this book, we'll be covering the ins and outs of how to shop, cook, and eat your way through the Mediterranean diet in the most practical, simple, and cost-effective way possible. And because everyone loves a bonus, you'll find a complete four-week meal plan to show you how easily doable and flavor rich the Mediterranean diet can be.

Before we dive straight into all the simple ways you can save money on your grocery bill, it's important first to understand what makes the Mediterranean diet so healthy in the first place.

5 Frugal Favorites

All the Mediterranean diet recipes you'll find in this cookbook are budget friendly and easy to prepare; here are my frugal favorites that stand above the rest:

Greek-Inspired Pasta Salad: Toss together whole wheat pasta with a can of tuna, chopped artichokes, crumbled feta cheese, and black olives. Lightly coat with homemade Lemony Greek Dressing (page 136) to tie everything together.

Greek Yogurt Bowl: Quick and easy for those busy mornings! Top a bowl of plain, low-fat Greek yogurt with warmed frozen blueberries, a handful of sliced walnuts, and a dash of cinnamon.

Grilled Chicken Wrap: Use leftover grilled chicken to wrap up a balanced meal in a minute. Layer thinly sliced red onion, chopped romaine lettuce, sliced cucumbers, grilled chicken, and a dollop of plain Greek yogurt, and roll it all up in a whole wheat wrap.

Hummus Platter: If you're in the mood for a snack plate kind of meal, this one's easy to pull together. Serve up Quick Garlic Hummus (page 134) with some whole-grain crackers, vegetable sticks, fresh grapes, and a side of dry-roasted nuts to satisfy all your cravings in one meal.

Vegetable Bean Soup: Great for using up those wilting veggies! Chop up whatever veggies you have on hand (such as carrots, celery, onion, squash, green beans, or kale), give them a quick sauté, then add low-sodium vegetable broth and a can or two of your favorite beans. Serve with a side of crusty whole-grain bread or a piece of fruit for a quick meal.

The Health Benefits of the Mediterranean Diet

Doctors, registered dietitians, and researchers agree: Following a Mediterranean-inspired dietary pattern can be beneficial to maintaining and even improving overall health. The following are some of the key areas of health and well-being that the Mediterranean diet can positively impact.

Cardiovascular Disease

Following the Mediterranean diet has some serious benefits for heart health. According to the Centers for Disease Control and Prevention (CDC), about 655,000 Americans die from heart disease each year, about one in every four deaths in the United States. There is growing evidence that adhering to a Mediterranean diet can help reduce the risk of coronary heart disease, stroke, and overall cardiovascular disease.

Diabetes

Diet and lifestyle can play a big part in the prevention and treatment of type 2 diabetes. Research has shown that adopting a Mediterranean diet can lower the risk of type 2 diabetes and help those with type 2 diabetes manage blood sugar levels. Furthermore, a Mediterranean diet can assist those with metabolic syndrome—a risk factor for type 2 diabetes—reduce the risk of developing diabetes by up to 23 percent.

High Blood Pressure

Hypertension or high blood pressure is one of the biggest risk factors for cardiovascular disease. There is evidence that the Mediterranean diet may help lower blood pressure for those with high blood pressure as well as healthy individuals. Some aspects of the diet, such as limiting high-sodium foods and focusing on fresh fruits, vegetables, and whole grains, play a role in its blood-pressure-lowering capabilities.

High Cholesterol

Another risk factor for developing heart disease is high cholesterol. More research is still needed, but current scientific evidence shows a Mediterranean diet can help lower total cholesterol and LDL (bad) cholesterol levels. The emphasis on fatty fish, olives, olive oils, and other healthy fats in the Mediterranean diet plays a role in the prevention of heart disease and high cholesterol.

Other Conditions

There is also growing evidence that a Mediterranean diet can play a role in improving other chronic health conditions. Some research has shown that following the Mediterranean diet can help slow the progression of cognitive decline, improve cognitive functioning, and minimize the progression of Alzheimer's disease. Additionally, adhering to a Mediterranean diet can reduce the overall risk of cancer.

The Mediterranean Diet Pyramid

This flipped food pyramid emphasizes the foods you should eat most often at the top, moderately in the middle, and sparingly at the bottom.

Fruits, Vegetables, Grains (mostly whole), Olive Oil, Beans, Nuts, Legumes and Seeds, Herbs and Spices
Base every meal on these foods

Fish and Seafood
Often, at least two times per week

Poultry, Eggs, Cheese, and Yogurt
Moderate portions,
daily to weekly

Meats and Sweets
Less often

Wine
in moderation

Water
Drink plenty

The Building Blocks of the Mediterranean Diet

The Mediterranean diet is primarily composed of many healthy foods eaten in larger amounts and more frequently. It also includes a smaller list of foods eaten in smaller amounts and less frequently (but are still considered a nourishing part of the diet) and some foods to save for special occasions.

Foods to Eat with Gusto

For most meals, striking a balance of fruits and vegetables, lean proteins, whole grains, and healthy fats is helpful for feeling satisfied and getting in the variety of nutrients your body needs to feel its best each day. Here are some examples for each category to get you started.

VEGETABLES AND FRUIT

A variety of colors means a variety of vitamins and minerals when it comes to fruits and vegetables. Add as much color to your meals as possible with options such as tomatoes, onions, apples, pears, citrus fruits, peppers, leafy greens, berries, eggplant, asparagus, and avocados.

NUTS AND SEEDS

Nuts and seeds provide fiber, protein, healthy fats, and micronutrients to power the body through the day. Favorites include almonds, pistachios, walnuts, hazelnuts, cashews, pumpkin seeds, and sunflower seeds.

OILY FISH AND SEAFOOD

Seafood and oily fish are rich sources of omega-3 fatty acids, the healthy fats that help support heart health. They also provide a good dose of protein and micronutrients in every bite. Some examples of oily or fatty fish include salmon, mackerel, sardines, anchovies, and herring. Other seafood sources you may want to include in your diet are shrimp, scallops, cod, haddock, mussels, and clams.

OLIVES AND OLIVE OIL

You can't mention the Mediterranean without thinking about olives. These briny fruits and the oils they produce are full of healthy, monounsaturated fats and anti-oxidants that can help support a healthy heart. Use extra-virgin olive oil as your primary oil for cooking, dressings, and marinades.

BEANS, LEGUMES, AND WHOLE GRAINS

The last core components of the Mediterranean diet are beans, legumes, and whole grains. Beans and legumes are plant-based sources of protein and, along with whole grains, are rich sources of dietary fiber to support heart and gut health. Some options are chickpeas, white beans, lentils, brown rice, whole wheat pasta, barley, and bulgur.

Foods to Enjoy in Moderation

Fruits, vegetables, whole grains, and healthy fats may get most of the limelight, but that doesn't mean there isn't any room for other foods on the Mediterranean diet. While they may be eaten less often, these foods can still be enjoyed.

RED MEAT

Animal protein, including beef, lamb, veal, and pork, is a rich source of minerals like iron, selenium, magnesium, and B vitamins. To keep saturated fats in check, opt for leaner cuts of red meat, such as lean ground beef, pork loin, and sirloin, and enjoy them for special occasions, or about once or twice a month.

WINE

Moderate wine drinking is often part of the Mediterranean diet, and wine is a source of antioxidants, such as polyphenols, that are linked to longevity and anti-inflammatory properties. According to the USDA Dietary Guidelines for Americans, moderate drinking is defined as two drinks per day for men and one drink per day for women. One serving of wine is 5 ounces.

SWEETS

Satisfying your sweet tooth is part of the Mediterranean diet, as well. Stick to single-serve portions like a piece of chocolate or an ice cream bar, or opt for a fruit-based treat like berries with whipped cream to keep portions in check. Save your favorite decadent treats for special occasions or once or twice a month.

Foods to Minimize

All foods can fit into a Mediterranean lifestyle, but a few categories are best kept to a minimum to help best support you on your health journey. These foods are often less-nutritious options that don't necessarily fall into the key areas of a Mediterranean diet.

REFINED GRAINS

Whole grains like oats and barley are rich in fiber, vitamins, and minerals, but refined grains offer much lower amounts of these health-supporting nutrients. Refined grains include white bread, pasta, rice, cereals, and crackers. Replace refined grains with their whole-grain counterparts whenever possible.

ADDED SUGARS

Enjoying the occasional sweet treat can be a part of your health journey but indulging in too much added sugar each day can leave less room for nutrient-dense options. Added sugars are any sweeteners added to a food or beverage that aren't naturally occurring. The USDA's dietary guidelines recommend no more than 10 percent of your daily calories come from added sugars.

PROCESSED MEATS

Processed meats are preserved by methods such as salting, canning, curing, or smoking. They include sausage, hot dogs, salami, bacon, and canned and smoked meats. Processed meats tend to be high in additives, preservatives, and sodium. The frequent inclusion of high-sodium foods in the diet can increase the risk of high blood pressure, stroke, and cardiovascular disease.

HIGH-SODIUM FOODS

In addition to processed meats, other foods can contain higher amounts of sodium, which can negatively impact cardiovascular health if eaten too frequently. High-sodium foods include canned soups, frozen meals, chips, pretzels, bread, and condiments such as salad dressing, soy sauce, and marinades.

The Keys to Saving Money on the Mediterranean Diet

The best way to maximize your food budget and still enjoy all the Mediterranean diet has to offer comes down to planning. These key strategies will help you shop for budget-friendly, Mediterranean-inspired ingredients with ease.

Shop with a Plan in Hand

One tip I can't share enough is to never shop without a grocery list. Writing down what you need helps you stay on track, buy only the items you truly need, and

WHAT TO DRINK ON THE MEDITERRANEAN DIET?

What you drink on the Mediterranean diet is just as important as what you eat. Here are a few tips to guide you to some healthy beverage choices.

Beer and Liquor: Moderate alcohol intake can be a part of the Mediterranean diet for those who choose to enjoy it. Moderate means one drink per day for women and two drinks per day for men.

Coffee and Tea: Both coffee and tea can offer heart-health benefits, such as reducing the risk of cardiovascular disease. The USDA dietary guidelines recommend that up to three to five cups per day can be a part of a balanced diet. Limit the amount of add-ins like heavy cream, syrups, or sweeteners.

Red Wine: Drinking red wine in moderation can be a part of the Mediterranean diet. This includes 2 (5-ounce) glasses a day for men, or 1 (5-ounce) glass a day for women.

Sodas and Sweetened Beverages: They can be tasty, but sodas and other sweetened beverages can quickly add unwanted calories and added sugars to your diet. Limit the number of sweetened beverages you consume or save them for a special occasion.

Water: Staying hydrated is important for your body to work properly and can also help you feel more energized. The US National Academies of Sciences, Engineering, and Medicine currently recommends about 11 cups of water per day for women and about 15 cups per day for men.

ultimately save money. Better yet, write down the recipes you are making for the week on your list, too, as a reminder. Take inventory of what you have on hand, and most important, don't forget your list!

Buy in Bulk

If you find there are ingredients you buy repeatedly or use in multiple recipes throughout the week, buying them in bulk can be a big money saver. For example, purchasing a bulk, 32-ounce container of Greek yogurt instead of the single-serving cups can save you up to 30 percent. This could mean taking a monthly trip to your local wholesale grocery to stock up or simply buying the bigger containers of your favorites.

Cans, Bags, and Bins

Canned and frozen foods can be just as nutritious as their fresh counterparts and are often a fraction of the price. To look for the best deal, compare the unit price of similar items (often the number in yellow on the price tag). The lower the unit price, the better the deal. If your grocery store has one, you can also shop the bulk section for staple ingredients like grains, nuts, seeds, and spices, which are often much cheaper than prepackaged ones.

Store Brands

Most grocery stores have their own line of food products that offer the same quality and flavor as national brands but often at a much lower price. This includes frozen fruits and vegetables, olive oil, vinegar, canned beans and vegetables, and whole grains such as oats, pasta, and brown rice.

Deals and Coupons

Using your grocery store's weekly sales ad or the coupons in your local paper can also help you make the most out of your grocery trip. Many times, ingredients commonly used in the Mediterranean diet are on sale or have coupons that can reduce your food bill. These include olives and olive oil, vinegar, meat and poultry, seafood, nuts and seeds, and canned beans and vegetables.

Grab What's in Season

Shopping with the seasons is not only good for your wallet but also good for the taste buds. Purchasing produce in season is often more affordable and is much fresher and more flavorful than other times during the year. This can mean filling up your menu with tomatoes, peaches, and berries during the summer and switching to hardy greens, apples, and squashes during the colder months.

GROCERY LIST

DAIRY & EGGS

☐ yogurt
☐ milk
☐ eggs

PRODUCE

☐ Cauliflower
☐ beets

PANTRY ITEMS

☐ olive oil
☐ quinoa
☐ chickpeas, canned.

FRUGAL MEDITERRANEAN DIET MEAL PLANS

Now that you are armed with tips for reaping the benefits of the Mediterranean diet on a budget, it's time to get cooking. In this chapter, we'll cover all you need to get started on your Mediterranean diet journey, including four weeks' worth of easy, inexpensive meal plans.

Stocking Your Healthy Kitchen

Before you start cooking the recipes in this cookbook, here are some staple ingredients you'll want to stock in your kitchen.

Refrigerator and Freezer Staples

A big portion of the recipes in this book focus on quality fresh and frozen ingredients you can find at almost any grocery store.

- ☐ Berries, frozen (blueberries, strawberries)
- ☐ Feta cheese, crumbled
- ☐ Goat cheese
- ☐ Greek yogurt, plain, low-fat
- ☐ Ground turkey, lean
- ☐ Leafy greens (baby spinach, arugula, kale)
- ☐ Lemons and limes
- ☐ Mushrooms (white button)
- ☐ Red onions
- ☐ Shrimp, frozen, peeled, deveined
- ☐ Tofu, firm
- ☐ Tomatoes

Pantry Staples

These recipes will also incorporate pantry ingredients that you may already have or some you may need to buy but will soon become a staple in your kitchen.

- ☐ Almonds, raw, sliced, unsalted
- ☐ Beans, canned, low-sodium
- ☐ Brown lentils
- ☐ Brown rice
- ☐ Canned fish (boneless, skinless salmon, tuna, sardines)
- ☐ Dried fruits (pitted dates, golden raisins, dried apricots)
- ☐ Pistachios, shelled, unsalted
- ☐ Quinoa
- ☐ Rolled oats
- ☐ Tomato paste
- ☐ Whole wheat bread
- ☐ Whole wheat pasta

Tools and Equipment

The recipes and meal plans in this book require some common kitchen tools and storage containers.

Baking sheets: Great for roasting vegetables and baking fish, meats, and poultry.

Can opener: A must for canned beans, vegetables, and fish.

Chef's knife: Allows you to chop, slice, and prepare fresh ingredients.

Cutting boards: To ensure food safety, keep one for raw fruits and vegetables and another for preparing raw meats, poultry, and seafood exclusively.

Glass storage containers: Excellent for storing leftovers while still being able to see what's inside.

Large mesh strainer: Useful for washing fruits and veggies and straining foods such as pasta and canned beans.

Mixing bowls: A variety of sizes is super helpful for preparing and serving dishes. I recommend a set of three with a 1.5-quart, 3-quart, and 5-quart bowl.

Nonstick skillet: Makes for easy cooking and cleanup, especially for eggs.

Pots with lids: Having at least a small, medium, and large pot makes preparing recipes according to yield easier.

Rubber spatula: Makes stirring and scraping otherwise messy ingredients a breeze.

Sauté pan: A deeper option than a skillet that comes in handy for sauteing vegetables, preparing sauces, and pasta dishes.

4 Weeks of Affordable Mediterranean Diet Meals

Following a simple meal plan is a great way to get into the Mediterranean diet's groove. The meal plans include 10 recipes per week for four weeks. They are intended for two people but can easily be adapted for one person or scaled up for a family of four. If cooking for one, consider making dishes that feed four at the beginning of the week to enjoy leftovers throughout the week or opt for more breakfast and snack recipes designed for smaller servings. If feeding a family, consider adding an extra dish or two or choosing recipes that feed four or six, especially for dinner.

While grocery prices vary throughout the country, generally, one person can expect to pay around $50 to $80 a week on this meal plan, while a family of four may spend up to $200 to $300.

Egg-Stuffed Portabella Mushrooms, **page 36**

Kale and Navy Bean Stew, **page 74**

Week 1

	BREAKFAST	LUNCH	DINNER	SNACK
1	Asparagus and Goat Cheese Egg Bites (page 39) 1 slice of whole-grain toast	Greek-Inspired Beef Pitas (page 111)	Moroccan-Inspired Tofu Quinoa Bowls (page 71)	Quick Garlic Hummus (page 134) with vegetable sticks
2	*Leftover Asparagus and Goat Cheese Egg Bites* 1 slice whole-grain toast	*Leftover Moroccan-Inspired Tofu Quinoa Bowls*	*Leftover Greek-Inspired Beef Pitas*	Plain low-fat Greek yogurt with blueberries and walnuts
3	*Leftover Asparagus and Goat Cheese Egg Bites* 1 slice whole-grain toast	One-Pot Rice and Beans (page 78)	Scallop Scampi with Crispy Shallots (page 88)	Savory Hummus Energy Bites (page 56)
4	Whole-grain toast with sliced avocado and a hard-boiled egg	*Leftover Scallop Scampi with Crispy Shallots*	*Leftover One-Pot Rice and Beans*	Banana with 1 ounce walnuts
5	Cherry Almond Breakfast Quinoa (page 42)	*Leftover One-Pot Rice and Beans*	Kale and Navy Bean Stew (page 74)	*Leftover Savory Hummus Energy Bites*
6	*Leftover Cherry Almond Breakfast Quinoa*	*Leftover Kale and Navy Bean Stew*	Harissa-Spiced Turkey Burgers with Tzatziki (page 107)	*Leftover Savory Hummus Energy Bites*
7	Whole-grain cereal with banana and walnuts	*Leftover Harissa-Spiced Turkey Burgers with Tzatziki*	*Leftover Kale and Navy Bean Stew*	Orange with 1 ounce almonds

MEAL PREP AHEAD OF TIME: Asparagus and Goat Cheese Egg Bites (page 39), Quick Garlic Hummus (page 134), Savory Hummus Energy Bites (page 56), One-Pot Rice and Beans (page 78)

Week 1 Shopping List

Each week I spent roughly $200 to $300, depending on which ingredients were on sale and which items I already had on hand. I used money-saving tips (see page 8), such as taking an inventory of my pantry, refrigerator, and freezer to see what items I already had on hand. Also, I used the sales flyer for my local grocery stores to help me decide on recipes for the week and compare unit pricing on items like Greek yogurt, cheese, and spices to get the most for my money. Most important, I brought my shopping list with me to the store and stuck to it. Taking a picture of it on my phone before I left was a big help.

PRODUCE

- ☐ Arugula (6 ounces)
- ☐ Asparagus (1 bunch)
- ☐ Avocado (1 large)
- ☐ Banana (2 large)
- ☐ Bell pepper, red (1 large)
- ☐ Carrot (4 large)
- ☐ Celery (2 stalks)
- ☐ Cilantro, fresh (1 bunch)
- ☐ Cucumber (2 large)
- ☐ Garlic (2 bulbs)
- ☐ Ginger, fresh (1 inch knob)
- ☐ Kale, chopped (16 ounces)
- ☐ Lemon (2 large)
- ☐ Onion, yellow (5 large)
- ☐ Orange (2 large)
- ☐ Parsley, fresh (1 bunch)
- ☐ Shallot (1 large)
- ☐ Tomato (2 large)

DAIRY AND EGGS

- ☐ Butter, unsalted (1 stick)
- ☐ Cheese, feta, crumbled (2 ounces)
- ☐ Cheese, goat (4 ounces)
- ☐ Cheese, Parmesan, grated (6 ounces)
- ☐ Eggs, large (12)
- ☐ Milk, low-fat (½ gallon)
- ☐ Yogurt, Greek, low-fat plain (1 [32-ounce] tub)

MEAT AND SEAFOOD

- ☐ Beef, ground, lean (1 pound)
- ☐ Turkey, ground, lean (1 pound)

FROZEN

- ☐ Blueberries
  (1 [12-ounce] bag)
- ☐ Cherries, sweet
  (1 [12-ounce] bag)
- ☐ Scallops, bay
  (1 pound)

HERBS AND SPICES

- ☐ Bay leaves
- ☐ Chili powder
- ☐ Cinnamon, ground
- ☐ Cumin, ground
- ☐ Dill, dried
- ☐ Harissa seasoning
- ☐ Italian seasoning
- ☐ Nutmeg, ground
- ☐ Oregano, dried
- ☐ Red pepper flakes
- ☐ Rosemary, dried
- ☐ Turmeric, ground

PANTRY

- ☐ Almonds, sliced
  (1 [10-ounce] bag)
- ☐ Almond extract
- ☐ Apricots, dried
  (1 [6-ounce] bag)
- ☐ Angel-hair pasta,
  whole wheat, dry
  (1 pound)
- ☐ Beans, cannellini
  (1 [28-ounce] can)
- ☐ Beans, navy
  (2 [15-ounce] cans)
- ☐ Beans, red kidney
  (1 [28-ounce] can)
- ☐ Broth, vegetable,
  low-sodium
- (4 [32-ounce]
  containers)
- ☐ Cereal, whole-grain
  (1 [10-ounce] box)
- ☐ Chickpeas
  (1 [28-ounce] can)
- ☐ Dijon mustard
- ☐ Honey
  (1 [4-ounce] jar)
- ☐ Italian bread crumbs
- ☐ Oats, rolled
  (18-ounce
  container)
- ☐ Pumpkin seeds,
  shelled (2 ounces)
- ☐ Quinoa, red
  (1 [16-ounce] bag)
- ☐ Rice, brown
  (1 pound)
- ☐ Sunflower seeds,
  shelled (2 ounces)
- ☐ Tomato paste
  (1 [6-ounce] can)
- ☐ Tomatoes, diced,
  low-sodium
  (2 [28-ounce] cans)
- ☐ Tomatoes,
  fire-roasted
  (1 [15-ounce] can)
- ☐ Vanilla extract
- ☐ Walnuts, chopped
  (1 [10-ounce] bag)

OTHER

- ☐ Bread, whole wheat (1 loaf)
- ☐ Hamburger buns, whole wheat (1 [12-ounce] package)
- ☐ Pita bread, whole wheat (1 [24-ounce] package)
- ☐ Tofu, extra-firm (1 [12-ounce] package)

Shakshuka Bake, *page 38*

Jeweled Rice, *page 64*

Week 2

	BREAKFAST	LUNCH	DINNER	SNACK
1	Shakshuka Bake (page 38)	Salad Niçoise with Mackerel (page 87)	Herbed Lamb Chops with Lemon-Rosemary Dressing (page 102)	Oven-Baked Pita Chips (page 58)
2	*Leftover Shakshuka Bake*	*Leftover Salad Niçoise with Mackerel*	*Leftover Herbed Lamb Chops with Lemon-Rosemary Dressing*	*Leftover Oven-Baked Pita Chips*
3	Whole-grain toast with nut butter and fruit	*Leftover Herbed Lamb Chops with Lemon-Rosemary Dressing*	Jeweled Rice (page 64)	Plain low-fat Greek yogurt with frozen berries
4	Peach and Pistachio Greek Yogurt Bowl (page 46)	*Leftover Jeweled Rice*	Salmon Patties with Dill Yogurt Sauce (page 91)	Herbed Feta Dip with Cucumber Slices (page 57)
5	Whole-grain cereal with piece of fruit	*Leftover Salmon Patties with Dill Yogurt Sauce*	*Leftover Jeweled Rice*	*Leftover Herbed Feta Dip with Cucumber Slices*
6	Peach and Pistachio Greek Yogurt Bowl (page 46)	Sun-Dried Tomato and Arugula Stuffed Chicken Breasts (page 104)	Spicy Pork and Zucchini Pasta (page 109)	Piece of fruit and nut butter
7	Oatmeal with frozen berries and almonds	*Leftover Spicy Pork and Zucchini Pasta*	*Leftover Sun-Dried Tomato and Arugula Stuffed Chicken Breasts*	Lightly salted popcorn

MEAL PREP AHEAD OF TIME: Oven-Baked Pita Chips (page 58), Herbed Feta Dip (page 57), Salmon Patties with Dill Yogurt Sauce (page 91)

Week 2 Shopping List

PRODUCE

- ☐ Apple (2 large)
- ☐ Arugula (10 ounces)
- ☐ Bell pepper, red (2 large)
- ☐ Carrots (2 large)
- ☐ Cilantro, fresh (1 bunch)
- ☐ Cucumbers (3 large)
- ☐ Garlic (1 bulb)
- ☐ Ginger, fresh (1 inch knob)
- ☐ Lemon (1 large)
- ☐ Lemon juice (1 bottle)
- ☐ Lettuce, romaine (2 heads)
- ☐ Orange (1 large)
- ☐ Onion, red (1 small)
- ☐ Onion, yellow (3 large)
- ☐ Parsley, fresh (1 bunch)
- ☐ Peaches (2 large)
- ☐ Potatoes, red-skinned (1 [1-pound] bag)
- ☐ Rosemary, fresh (1 bunch)
- ☐ Shallots (2 large)
- ☐ Tomatoes, cherry (1 pint)
- ☐ Zucchini (2 medium)

DAIRY AND EGGS

- ☐ Cheese, feta, crumbled (6 ounces)
- ☐ Cheese, Parmesan, grated (4 ounces)
- ☐ Eggs, large (1½ dozen)
- ☐ Milk, low-fat (1 pint)
- ☐ Yogurt, Greek, low-fat plain (2 [32-ounce] tub)

MEAT AND SEAFOOD

- ☐ Chicken, breasts, boneless, skinless (4 pack)
- ☐ Lamb, chops (6 [1-inch-thick] pieces)
- ☐ Pork, ground, lean (1 pound)

FROZEN

- ☐ Berries, mixed (10 ounces)
- ☐ Green beans (12 ounces)
- ☐ Peas and carrots (8 ounces)

HERBS AND SPICES

- ☐ Cardamom, ground
- ☐ Cayenne pepper
- ☐ Cinnamon, ground
- ☐ Cumin, ground
- ☐ Dill, dried
- ☐ Garlic powder
- ☐ Italian seasoning
- ☐ Oregano, dried
- ☐ Paprika
- ☐ Red pepper flakes
- ☐ Turmeric, ground

PANTRY

- Almonds, sliced
  (1 [10-ounce] bag)
- Cereal, whole-grain
  (1 [10-ounce] box)
- Cranberries, dried
  (1 [10-ounce] bag)
- Dijon mustard
  (1 [12-ounce] jar)
- Honey
  (1 [4-ounce] jar)
- Italian bread crumbs
  (1 [15-ounce]
  canister)
- Mackerel, boneless,
  skinless, canned
  in water
  (2 [5-ounce] cans)

- Nut butter or
  peanut butter
  (1 [16-ounce] jar)
- Oats, rolled
  (1 [18-ounce]
  canister)
- Olives, kalamata
  (1 [7-ounce] jar)
- Pistachios, shelled,
  unsalted
  (1 [3-ounce] bag)
- Popcorn,
  lightly salted
  (1 [4-ounce] bag)
- Rice, basmati
  (1 [1-pound] bag)

- Rotini, whole wheat
  (1 pound)
- Salmon, boneless,
  skinless
  (1 [15-ounce] can)
- Sun-dried tomatoes
  (1 [6-ounce] jar)
- Tomatoes, diced,
  low-sodium
  (1 [28-ounce] can)
- Tomatoes,
  fire-roasted, diced
  (1 [15-ounce] can)
- Tomatoes, stewed
  (1 [15-ounce] can)
- Vinegar, red wine
  (1 [16-ounce] bottle)

OTHER

- Bread, whole wheat
  (1 loaf)

- Pita bread, whole
  wheat (1 [12-ounce]
  package)

Creamy Melon Mint Smoothie, *page 47*

Tomato and Basil Bruschetta, *page 50*

Week 3

	BREAKFAST	LUNCH	DINNER	SNACK
1	Egg-Stuffed Portabella Mushrooms (page 36)	Roasted Cauliflower Tagine (page 67) with couscous	Tzatziki Pork Chops (page 108) with steamed vegetable	Apple with nut butter
2	*Leftover Egg-Stuffed Portabella Mushrooms*	*Leftover Tzatziki Pork Chops with steamed vegetables*	*Leftover Roasted Cauliflower Tagine with couscous*	Tomato and Basil Bruschetta (page 50)
3	Creamy Melon Mint Smoothie (page 47)	*Leftover Roasted Cauliflower Tagine with couscous*	*Leftover Tzatziki Pork Chops*	*Leftover Tomato and Basil Bruschetta*
4	Lemon Ricotta Toast with Blueberry Compote (page 45)	Steak and Swiss Chard Sandwiches with Roasted Garlic Sauce (page 113)	Za'atar Roasted Chicken Thighs (page 103) with steamed vegetables	Whole-grain crackers with 1 ounce cheese
5	*Leftover Lemon Ricotta Toast with Blueberry Compote*	*Leftover Za'atar Roasted Chicken Thighs with steamed vegetables*	*Leftover Steak and Swiss Chard Sandwiches with Roasted Garlic Sauce*	Blue Cheese and Walnut Stuffed Dates (page 60)
6	Whole-grain cereal with banana	*Leftover Steak and Swiss Chard Sandwiches with Roasted Garlic Sauce*	*Leftover Za'atar Roasted Chicken Thighs with steamed vegetables*	*Leftover Blue Cheese and Walnut Stuffed Dates*
7	Oatmeal with walnuts and raisins	Open-Faced Caprese Tuna Melts (page 85)	Spaghetti with Tomatoes and Sardines (page 95)	2 hard-boiled eggs

MEAL PREP AHEAD OF TIME: Egg-Stuffed Portabella Mushrooms (page 36), Blueberry Compote (page 45), Easy Tzatziki (page 140), Roasted Garlic (page 135)

Week 3 Shopping List

PRODUCE

- ☐ Apple (1 large)
- ☐ Banana (2 large)
- ☐ Basil, fresh (1 bunch)
- ☐ Bell pepper, red (1 large)
- ☐ Carrots (4 large)
- ☐ Cauliflower (2 heads)
- ☐ Cilantro, fresh (1 bunch)
- ☐ Cucumbers (1 large)
- ☐ Garlic (2 bulbs)
- ☐ Honeydew melon (1)
- ☐ Lemon (4 large)
- ☐ Lemon juice (1 [8-ounce] bottle)
- ☐ Lime (1 large)
- ☐ Mint, fresh (1 bunch)
- ☐ Mushrooms, portabella (4 large)
- ☐ Onion, red (1 large)
- ☐ Onion, sweet (4 large)
- ☐ Parsley, fresh (1 bunch)
- ☐ Potatoes (3 large russet)
- ☐ Swiss chard (1 bunch)
- ☐ Tomatoes (4 large)

DAIRY AND EGGS

- ☐ Cheese, blue (3 ounces)
- ☐ Cheese, mozzarella, fresh (8 ounces)
- ☐ Cheese, Parmesan, grated (4 ounces)
- ☐ Cheese, ricotta, part-skim (16 ounces)
- ☐ Eggs, large (1 dozen)
- ☐ Milk, low-fat (1 quart)
- ☐ Yogurt, Greek, low-fat plain (1 [32-ounce] tub)

MEAT AND SEAFOOD

- ☐ Beef, sirloin tip roast (1½ pounds)
- ☐ Chicken, boneless, skinless thighs (6 pack)
- ☐ Pork, chops, thin-cut (6 pack)

FROZEN

- ☐ Blueberries (1 [16-ounce] bag)
- ☐ Vegetable medley (4 [12 ounce] bags)

HERBS AND SPICES

☐ Coriander, ground

☐ Dill, dried

☐ Garlic powder

☐ Italian seasoning

☐ Red pepper flakes

☐ Za'atar seasoning

PANTRY

☐ Capers
(1 [4-ounce] jar)

☐ Cereal, whole-grain
(1 [10-ounce] box)

☐ Chickpeas
(1 [15-ounce] can)

☐ Couscous
(1 [10-ounce] box)

☐ Crackers,
whole-grain
(1 [10-ounce] box)

☐ Dates, pitted
(1 [10-ounce] bag)

☐ Dijon mustard
(1 [10-ounce] jar)

☐ Nut butter or
peanut butter
(1 [16-ounce] jar)

☐ Oats, rolled
(1 [18-ounce]
container)

☐ Olives, black, sliced
(1 [4-ounce] can)

☐ Raisins
(1 [12-ounce] box)

☐ Sardines, bone-
less, skinless in
tomato sauce
(2 [4-ounce] cans)

☐ Spaghetti,
whole wheat
[16-ounce box]

☐ Tomato paste
(1 [6-ounce] can)

☐ Tomatoes, diced,
low-sodium
(2 [28-ounce] cans)

☐ Tuna, chunk white
(2 [5-ounce] cans)

☐ Vinegar, balsamic
(1 [16-ounce] bottle)

☐ Walnut halves
(1 [10-ounce] bag)

☐ Worcester-
shire sauce
(1 [10-ounce] bottle)

OTHER

☐ Baguette (1)

☐ Bread, whole wheat
(1 loaf)

☐ Hamburger buns,
whole wheat
(pack of 6)

Savory Tomato Parmesan Oatmeal, **page 41**

Quick Garlic Hummus, **page 134**

Week 4

	BREAKFAST	LUNCH	DINNER	SNACK
1	Savory Tomato Parmesan Oatmeal (page 41)	Crab-Stuffed Portabella Mushrooms (page 93)	Marinated Pork Loin with Olive Tapenade (page 110)	Oven-Baked Pita Chips (page 58) with Quick Garlic Hummus (page 134)
2	Plain low-fat Greek yogurt with apple and walnuts	*Leftover Marinated Pork Loin with Olive Tapenade*	*Leftover Crab-Stuffed Portabella Mushrooms*	Lightly salted popcorn & a handful of walnuts
3	Mediterranean-Inspired Breakfast Sandwich (page 44)	Bulgur and Turkey Stuffed Zucchini (page 106)	Lamb and Mushroom Meatballs with Yogurt Sauce (page 100)	Savory Hummus Energy Bites (page 56)
4	*Leftover Savory Tomato Parmesan Oatmeal*	*Leftover Lamb and Mushroom Meatballs with Yogurt Sauce*	*Leftover Bulgur and Turkey Stuffed Zucchini*	Apple with nut butter
5	Whole wheat toast with sliced avocado and feta cheese	*Leftover Bulgur and Turkey Stuffed Zucchini*	Spiced Ground Beef and Eggplant Couscous Bowls (page 114)	*Leftover Savory Hummus Energy Bites*
6	Mediterranean-Inspired Breakfast Sandwich (page 44)	*Leftover Spiced Ground Beef and Eggplant Couscous Bowls*	Citrus-Poached Cod (page 94)	*Leftover Savory Hummus Energy Bites*
7	2 hard-boiled eggs + apple	Smashed Lentil Salad with Avocado and Feta (page 70)	*Leftover Citrus-Poached Cod*	*Leftover Oven-Baked Pita Chips with Hummus*

MEAL PREP AHEAD OF TIME: Oven-Baked Pita Chips (page 58), Quick Garlic Hummus (page 134), Savory Hummus Energy Bites (page 56), Smashed Lentil Salad with Avocado and Feta (page 70)

Week 4 Shopping List

PRODUCE

- ☐ Apple (3 large)
- ☐ Arugula (6 ounces)
- ☐ Avocado (3 large)
- ☐ Basil, fresh (1 bunch)
- ☐ Bell pepper, red (2 large)
- ☐ Carrot (1 large)
- ☐ Eggplant (1 large)
- ☐ Garlic (2 bulbs)
- ☐ Lemon (4 large)
- ☐ Lime (1 large)
- ☐ Mint, fresh (1 bunch)
- ☐ Mushrooms, button (8 ounces)
- ☐ Mushrooms, portabella (6 large)
- ☐ Onion, red (1 small)
- ☐ Onion, yellow (4 large)
- ☐ Orange (2 large)
- ☐ Parsley, fresh (1 bunch)
- ☐ Spinach, baby (6 ounces)
- ☐ Tomato (1 large)
- ☐ Zucchini (6 large)

DAIRY AND EGGS

- ☐ Eggs, large (1 dozen)
- ☐ Cheese, feta, crumbles (8 ounces)
- ☐ Cheese, Parmesan, grated (8 ounces)
- ☐ Yogurt, Greek, low-fat plain (1 [32-ounce] tub)

MEAT AND SEAFOOD

- ☐ Beef, ground, lean (1 pound)
- ☐ Cod, fillets, skinless (4)
- ☐ Lamb, ground (1 pound)
- ☐ Pork, loin chops, boneless (4)
- ☐ Turkey, ground, lean (1 pound)

HERBS AND SPICES

- ☐ Cinnamon, ground
- ☐ Cumin, ground
- ☐ Dill, dried
- ☐ Garlic powder
- ☐ Italian seasoning
- ☐ Nutmeg, ground
- ☐ Oregano, dried
- ☐ Paprika

PANTRY

- ☐ Broth, chicken, low-sodium [2 [32-ounce] cartons)
- ☐ Bulgur (1 [8-ounce] bag)
- ☐ Capers (1 [3-ounce] jar)
- ☐ Chickpeas, canned (1 [28-ounce] can)
- ☐ Couscous (1 [12-ounce] box)
- ☐ Crabmeat, white (2 [10-ounce] cans)
- ☐ Dijon mustard (1 [10-ounce] jar)

- ☐ Honey (1 [6 ounce] jar)
- ☐ Italian bread crumbs (1 [15-ounce] canister)
- ☐ Lentils, brown (2 [15-ounce] cans)
- ☐ Nut butter or peanut butter (1 [16-ounce] jar)
- ☐ Oats, rolled (1 [18-ounce] canister)
- ☐ Olives, black, sliced (1 [12-ounce] can)
- ☐ Olives, kalamata (1 [12-ounce] jar)

- ☐ Popcorn, lightly salted (1 [4-ounce] bag)
- ☐ Pumpkin seeds, shelled (4 ounces)
- ☐ Sunflower seeds, shelled (4 ounces)
- ☐ Tomato paste (1 [6-ounce] can)
- ☐ Tomatoes, diced, low-sodium (2 [15-ounce] cans)
- ☐ Vinegar, red wine (1 [12-ounce] bottle)
- ☐ Walnuts, chopped (1 [8-ounce] bag)

OTHER

- ☐ Bread, whole wheat (1 loaf)

- ☐ Pita bread, whole wheat (1 [12-ounce] bag)

The Recipes in This Book

The recipes you'll find in the following chapters are simple, affordable, and easy to follow. They can be enjoyed on their own or as a part of the meal plans. These nutritious recipes were designed and developed with ease of use in mind. That's why you'll find labels to indicate which recipes can be made in one-pot (or pan), with 5 or fewer ingredients (not counting the basics like salt, pepper, and olive oil), or in 30 minutes or less.

Labels will indicate whether a recipe is vegetarian or dairy-free. You'll also find nutrition information per serving for all recipes, along with tips for ingredient substitutions, variations, or shopping tips that make each recipe even easier to follow or adapt to meet your needs.

Best of all, these dishes are downright delicious. That's what we're here for, right? I hope these flavorful and budget-friendly recipes will inspire you on your Mediterranean diet journey and keep you coming back for more for years to come.

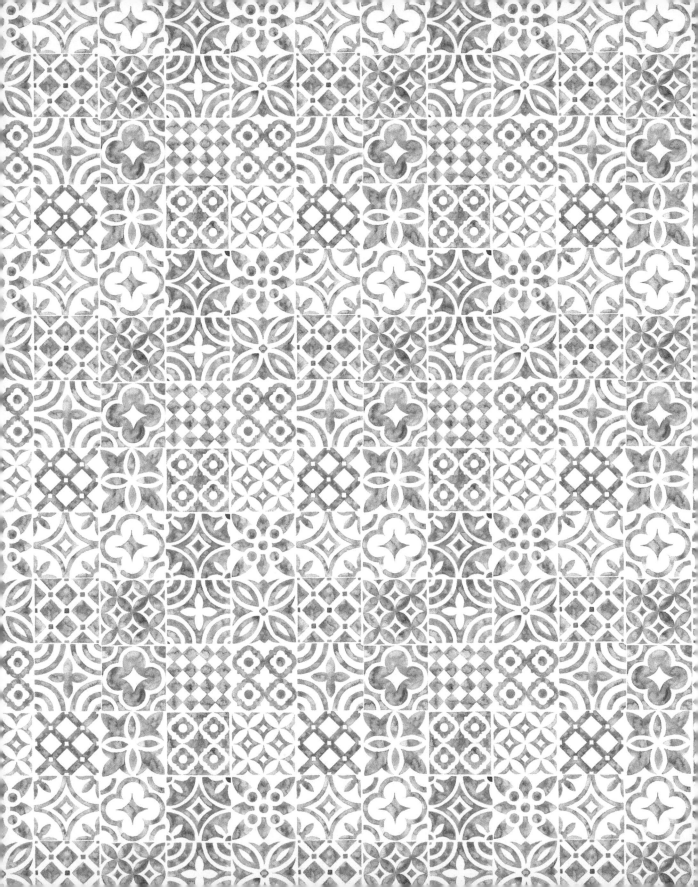

Shakshuka Bake, page 38

3

BREAKFAST

EGG-STUFFED PORTABELLA MUSHROOMS

Serves 4 / Prep time: 10 minutes / **Cook time:** 15 minutes

DAIRY-FREE, QUICK, VEGETARIAN

In this quick and easy breakfast recipe from dietitian Susan Zogheib, portabella mushrooms act as nature's edible cup. Not only are they a perfect vehicle for anti-inflammatory vegetables and flavor-rich eggs, but they are also a good source of energy-boosting B vitamins and important minerals like potassium and selenium, which can support heart health.

4 large portabella
   mushrooms
2 tablespoons extra-virgin
   olive oil, divided
Salt
Freshly ground black
   pepper
1 sweet onion, chopped
½ red bell pepper, seeded
   and finely chopped
1 teaspoon minced garlic
1 cup shredded Swiss
   chard
6 large eggs, beaten
1 tablespoon chopped
   fresh parsley

1. Preheat the oven to 425°F.

2. Remove the stems and scoop the black gills out of the mushrooms, creating a deep well. Rub the mushrooms with 1 tablespoon of oil and season with salt and pepper.

3. Place the mushrooms gill-side up on a baking sheet and roast until the mushrooms are tender, about 10 minutes.

4. While the mushrooms are baking, in a large skillet, heat the remaining 1 tablespoon of oil, and sauté the onion, bell pepper, and garlic over medium heat until softened, about 4 minutes.

5. Add the Swiss chard and sauté until wilted, about 4 minutes.

6. Stir in the eggs and scramble for about 4 minutes, until cooked through but still moist.

7. Spoon the eggs into the mushrooms, sprinkle parsley over the top, and serve.

INGREDIENT TIP: Portabella mushrooms should be dry, both top and gills. You can chop the gills up along with any scooped-out flesh and add it to the egg filling, but the black gills will tint the eggs an unappetizing gray.

Per Serving (1 stuffed mushroom): Calories: 206; Fat: 15g; Protein: 13g; Carbohydrates: 8g; Fiber: 2g; Sugar: 3g; Sodium: 180mg

SHAKSHUKA BAKE

Serves 4 / Prep time: 5 minutes / **Cook time:** 20 minutes

ONE-POT, QUICK, VEGETARIAN

Inspired by the popular dish in both Israeli and North African cooking, this shakshuka (*shack-shoo-kah*) recipe by dietitian Christine Patorniti is fit for breakfast, brunch, or even dinner. Eggs are a super affordable and versatile protein and are also a source of fat-soluble vitamins A, D, and E, which are important for eye and bone health.

1 tablespoon extra-virgin olive oil

1 cup chopped yellow onion

1 cup chopped red bell pepper

3 garlic cloves, minced

1 (28-ounce) can diced tomatoes

1 teaspoon ground cumin

1 teaspoon paprika

⅛ teaspoon cayenne pepper (optional)

8 large eggs

½ cup crumbled feta cheese

¼ cup chopped fresh cilantro

1. Preheat the oven to 350°F.

2. In an oven-safe large sauté pan or skillet, heat the oil over medium-high heat and sauté the onion, stirring occasionally, for about 3 minutes, or until fragrant.

3. Add the bell pepper and cook, uncovered, for 8 minutes, stirring occasionally. Add the garlic and cook for another 30 seconds.

4. Add the tomatoes, cumin, paprika, and cayenne pepper (if using) to the skillet and mix well. Once bubbling, remove from the heat and make 8 wells around the pan with the back of a spoon. Crack an egg into each well, and sprinkle feta cheese over the top.

5. Put the skillet in the oven and cook for 5 to 10 minutes, or until the eggs are cooked to your liking. Garnish with the cilantro and serve as is, or with a side of crusty whole-grain bread.

VARIATION TIP: Not a feta fan? Leave it out for a dairy-free option or use crumbled goat cheese instead.

Per Serving: Calories: 224; Total fat: 12g; Protein: 9g; Carbohydrates: 20g; Fiber: 3g; Sugar: 7g; Sodium: 278mg

ASPARAGUS AND GOAT CHEESE EGG BITES

Serves 6 / Prep time: 10 minutes / **Cook time:** 20 minutes, plus 5 minutes to rest

ONE-POT, VEGETARIAN

These egg bites are one of my favorite breakfasts to make ahead on a Sunday and enjoy throughout the week. Take advantage of seasonal sales on asparagus in the spring and summer for extra savings and opt for frozen in the fall and winter. Mixing eggs in a large liquid measuring cup makes pouring them into the muffin tin super easy and mess-free.

Nonstick cooking spray

2 cups finely chopped asparagus

10 large eggs

½ cup low-fat milk

2 garlic cloves, minced

¼ teaspoon salt

⅛ teaspoon ground nutmeg

4 ounces (about ½ cup) crumbled goat cheese

1. Preheat the oven to 350°F. Coat a 12-cup muffin tin with cooking spray.

2. Evenly divide the chopped asparagus between the cups and set the tin aside.

3. In a large liquid measuring cup, combine the eggs, milk, garlic, salt, and nutmeg.

4. Fill each muffin cup with an equal amount of the egg mixture, and sprinkle crumbled goat cheese over the top of each one.

5. Bake for 18 to 20 minutes, or until eggs are set.

6. Let rest for 5 minutes before removing the egg bites from the muffin tin and serving.

7. Refrigerate the leftovers in an airtight container for up to 5 days or freeze for up to 2 weeks.

INGREDIENT TIP: Look for a block of goat cheese and crumble it yourself at home. The pre-crumbled varieties tend to be a bit pricier.

Per Serving (2 egg bites): Calories: 188; Fat: 12g; Protein: 16g; Carbohydrates: 4g; Fiber: 1g; Sugar: 2g; Sodium: 312mg

SAVORY TOMATO PARMESAN OATMEAL

Serves 4 / Prep time: 5 minutes / **Cook time:** 20 minutes

QUICK

So, you thought oatmeal was just a vehicle for brown sugar and cinnamon? Let me introduce you to the savory side of this humble grain. This fiber- and protein-rich dish will change how you think about oatmeal forever. If enjoying leftovers, cook the egg just before eating for the best flavor and texture.

4 cups water

2 cups rolled oats

1 cup low-sodium diced
   tomatoes

2 garlic cloves, minced

1 teaspoon Italian
   seasoning

½ cup grated Parmesan
   cheese, divided

Nonstick cooking spray

4 large eggs

4 teaspoons extra-virgin
   olive oil

1. In a large pot, heat the water and oats over high heat until boiling.

2. Once boiling, reduce the heat to medium-low, and simmer for 10 minutes, stirring occasionally, until most of the water is absorbed.

3. Stir in the tomatoes, garlic, Italian seasoning, and ¼ cup of Parmesan cheese. Reduce the heat to low.

4. Coat a large nonstick skillet with cooking spray. Over medium-high heat, fry the eggs to desired consistency, 3 to 4 minutes for sunny-side up, 5 to 7 minutes for over easy or medium.

5. Divide the oatmeal between four bowls and sprinkle an equal amount of Parmesan cheese over each serving.

6. Top each serving with a fried egg and drizzle with oil before serving.

7. Refrigerate leftovers in an airtight container for up to 4 days. Reheat leftover oats for 1 to 2 minutes in the microwave and top with a freshly fried egg.

VARIATION TIP: If you have a garden full of basil, or if basil happens to be on sale, replace the Italian seasoning with chopped basil for a bright and fresh flavor.

Per Serving (1 bowl of savory oatmeal with one egg):
Calories: 349; Fat: 16g; Protein: 18g; Carbohydrates: 35g; Fiber: 6g; Sugar: 1g; Sodium: 300mg

CHERRY ALMOND BREAKFAST QUINOA

Serves 4 / Prep time: 5 minutes / **Cook time:** 20 minutes, plus 5 minutes to rest

ONE-POT, QUICK, VEGETARIAN

Just like oatmeal doesn't have to be sweet, quinoa doesn't have to be savory. I love the flavor combination of cherry and almonds. This hearty dish is especially satisfying on a chilly morning, and starting your day off with a bowl of this breakfast quinoa fuels you up with fiber, protein, and extra antioxidants from the almonds and cherries.

2 cups low-fat milk

1 cup rinsed red quinoa

1½ cups frozen sweet
   cherries

⅓ teaspoon almond extract

¼ teaspoon vanilla extract

¼ teaspoon ground
   cinnamon

½ cup sliced almonds

1. In a large pot, combine the milk and quinoa, and cook over medium-high heat until it starts to boil.

2. Reduce the heat to medium-low, and simmer for 15 to 20 minutes, or until the milk has been absorbed. Stir in the cherries in the last minute of cooking.

3. Remove the pot from the heat, cover, and let the quinoa sit for 5 minutes.

4. Stir in the almond extract, vanilla, cinnamon, and almonds before serving.

5. Refrigerate in an airtight container for up to 4 days.

SUBSTITUTION TIP: To make this dairy-free, substitute your favorite nondairy milk for the low-fat milk.

Per Serving: Calories: 322; Fat: 11g; Protein: 13g; Carbohydrates: 45g; Fiber: 6g; Sugar: 14g; Sodium: 60mg

SPICY CHOCOLATE OVERNIGHT OATS

Serves 4 / Prep time: 5 minutes, plus 4 hours to refrigerate

ONE-POT, VEGETARIAN

Overnight oats are the ultimate make-ahead breakfast. This recipe takes its flavor inspiration from spicy hot chocolate from Mexico. It's a chocolate lover's dream. Try this the next time you want to add a little kick to your morning routine.

4 cups skim milk

2 cups rolled oats

1 cup low-fat plain Greek
yogurt

¼ cup cocoa powder

1 tablespoon honey

1 teaspoon ground
cinnamon

¼ to ½ teaspoon chili
powder

1. In a large bowl, combine the milk, oats, yogurt, cocoa powder, honey, cinnamon, and chili powder, and mix thoroughly.

2. Divide the oat mixture between four containers with lids, cover, and refrigerate for at least 4 hours or overnight.

3. Before serving, stir, and pour in additional milk, if needed, for desired consistency.

VARIATION TIP: If you want a little extra kick, add a dash of cayenne pepper to your oats.

Per Serving (1 container): Calories: 337; Fat: 5g; Protein: 20g; Carbohydrates: 55g; Fiber: 7g; Sugar: 21g; Sodium: 165mg

MEDITERRANEAN-INSPIRED BREAKFAST SANDWICH

Serves 2 / **Prep time:** 10 minutes / **Cook time:** 5 minutes

DAIRY-FREE, QUICK, VEGETARIAN

If you're not an egg fan but still want a super-satisfying and portable breakfast, you've come to the right place. Each sandwich is piled high with garlicky spinach, fiber-rich avocado, and a healthy dollop of hummus to hold it all together. What's not to love?

1 teaspoon extra-virgin
  olive oil

2 cups baby spinach

1 garlic clove, minced

4 slices whole-grain bread,
  or 2 whole wheat English
  muffins

¼ cup Quick Garlic
  Hummus (page 134) or
  store-bought hummus

2 tablespoons sliced black
  olives

½ avocado, sliced

1. In a large skillet, heat the oil over medium heat.

2. Add the spinach and garlic and cook for 5 minutes, or until the spinach has wilted.

3. Lay out 2 slices of bread and spread 2 tablespoons of the hummus on each one. Top each piece of hummus-covered bread with half the cooked spinach and a tablespoon of sliced olives.

4. Add the sliced avocado to each sandwich and top with remaining bread slices before serving.

VARIATION TIP: Not a spinach fan? Swap it out for chopped kale or arugula instead.

Per Serving (1 sandwich): Calories: 332; Fat: 15g; Protein: 11g; Carbohydrates: 36g; Fiber: 10g; Sugar: 4g; Sodium: 372mg

LEMON RICOTTA TOAST WITH BLUEBERRY COMPOTE

Serves 4 / Prep time: 5 minutes / **Cook time:** 10 minutes

QUICK, VEGETARIAN

Step aside, avocado; there's a new toast topper in town. The combination of creamy ricotta and saucy, warm blueberries is such a wonderful flavor and texture experience that this is sure to become a regular part of your breakfast rotation.

2 cups part-skim ricotta cheese

2 teaspoons grated lemon zest

2 teaspoons freshly squeezed lemon juice

2 cups frozen blueberries

2 tablespoons water

2 tablespoons balsamic vinegar

4 slices whole wheat bread

1. In a small bowl, combine the ricotta, lemon zest, and lemon juice, and set aside.

2. In a medium saucepan, cook the blueberries, water, and balsamic vinegar over medium heat until the mixture comes to a boil.

3. Once boiling, reduce heat to medium-low, and continue to cook for an additional 5 to 8 minutes, or until thickened.

4. Remove the blueberry mixture from the heat and toast the bread.

5. Top each slice of bread with the ricotta mixture and the blueberry compote before serving.

6. Refrigerate leftover ricotta and blueberry compote in separate airtight containers for up to 4 days. Serve leftovers over freshly toasted bread.

VARIATION TIP: Top each toast with fresh basil or mint for extra depth of flavor.

Per Serving (1 piece of toast topped with lemon ricotta and blueberry compote): Calories: 299; Fat: 11g; Protein: 18g; Carbohydrates: 31g; Fiber: 4g; Sugar: 10g; Sodium: 271mg

PEACH AND PISTACHIO GREEK YOGURT BOWL

Serves 2 / Prep time: 10 minutes

5 INGREDIENTS OR FEWER, ONE-POT, QUICK, VEGETARIAN

When you're short on time, this quick, protein-rich yogurt bowl is an easy breakfast option to power you through even the busiest of mornings. Pistachios add crunch and heart-healthy fats, as well as key nutrients such as potassium and fiber, first thing in the morning.

1½ cups low-fat plain Greek yogurt

1 peach, pitted and chopped

½ cup dried cranberries

¼ cup unsalted, shelled pistachios

½ teaspoon ground cinnamon

1. Divide the yogurt evenly between two serving bowls.

2. Top each bowl with half of the peach and the cranberries, pistachios, and cinnamon, and serve.

SUBSTITUTION TIP: Replace the peach with seasonal fruit such as apples, strawberries, or grapefruit slices to take advantage of sales throughout the year.

Per Serving (¾ cup yogurt topped with fruit and nuts):
Calories: 333; Fat: 10g; Protein: 14g; Carbohydrates: 51g; Fiber: 4g; Sugar: 40g; Sodium: 131mg

CREAMY MELON MINT SMOOTHIE

Serves 2 / Prep time: 5 minutes

ONE-POT, QUICK, VEGETARIAN

This smoothie is pure refreshment in a glass. The honeydew and banana add potassium and vitamin C, and their natural sweetness balances the refreshing bite of fresh mint. Feel free to add a touch of honey, depending on the ripeness and sweetness of the melon.

3 cups chopped ripe
honeydew melon

1 frozen ripe banana

½ cup low-fat plain Greek
yogurt

½ cup low-fat milk

2 tablespoons chopped
fresh mint leaves

1 tablespoon freshly
squeezed lime juice

1. Put the melon, banana, yogurt, milk, mint, and lime juice into a blender, and blend on high for 1 minute, or until creamy.

2. Divide between two glasses and serve.

SUBSTITUTION TIP: Replace the yogurt and milk with plant-based alternatives to make this smoothie dairy-free.

Per Serving (1½ cups): Calories: 213; Fat: 3g; Protein: 6g; Carbohydrates: 44g; Fiber: 4g; Sugar: 35g; Sodium: 104mg

Skillet Asparagus with Lemon Zest and Red Pepper Flakes, **page 52**

SIDES AND SNACKS

TOMATO AND BASIL BRUSCHETTA

Serves 4 / Prep time: 15 minutes / **Cook time:** 5 minutes

5 INGREDIENTS OR FEWER, DAIRY-FREE, QUICK, VEGETARIAN

Bruschetta may sound fancy, but it couldn't be easier to prepare. Serve it up for an afternoon snack or a simple appetizer, especially when tomatoes are in season. You can even make a shortcut version with canned diced tomatoes (be sure to drain them) when tomatoes aren't fresh or are too expensive.

½ baguette, cut into 12 slices

1 tablespoon extra-virgin olive oil

2 large ripe tomatoes, seeded and chopped

1 cup chopped fresh basil

2 garlic cloves, minced

½ teaspoon balsamic vinegar

Salt

Freshly ground black pepper

1. Preheat the oven to 450°F.

2. Brush the bread slices with oil and place them oil-side down on a baking sheet. Set aside.

3. In a small bowl, combine the tomatoes, basil, garlic, and balsamic vinegar. Season with salt and pepper to taste.

4. Toast the bread for 3 to 5 minutes, or until crisp and lightly toasted. Remove the bread from the oven, top each piece with 1 tablespoon of the tomato mixture, and serve.

Per Serving (3 pieces of bruschetta): Calories: 206; Fat: 8g; Protein: 6g; Carbohydrates: 28g; Fiber: 2g; Sugar: 5g; Sodium: 313mg

SKILLET ASPARAGUS WITH LEMON ZEST AND RED PEPPER FLAKES

Serves 4 / **Prep time:** 10 minutes / **Cook time:** 10 minutes

5 INGREDIENTS OR FEWER, DAIRY-FREE, QUICK, VEGETARIAN

I love the bright, fresh flavor of asparagus, and adding a bit of fresh lemon and red pepper flakes is a simple way to take the taste up a notch. This easy side dish inspired by cookbook authors Kenton and Jane Kotsiris is quick to prepare any night of the week, and it can even be made with frozen asparagus in a pinch. Cooking time may vary if using frozen.

¼ **cup extra-virgin olive oil**

2 **pounds asparagus, woody ends trimmed**

3 **garlic cloves, minced**

Grated zest of 1 lemon

¼ **teaspoon red pepper flakes**

2 **teaspoons freshly squeezed lemon juice**

Salt

Freshly ground black pepper

1. In a large skillet, heat the oil over medium-high heat. Add the asparagus, stir to coat it with the oil, and sauté for 3 minutes.

2. Add the garlic, lemon zest, and red pepper flakes. Sauté for 5 to 7 minutes more, or until the asparagus is tender.

3. Stir in the lemon juice, and season with salt and pepper to taste before serving.

VARIATION TIP: Add a bit of crunch by stirring in ¼ cup of sliced almonds before serving.

Per Serving: Calories: 171; Total fat: 14g; Total carbs: 10g; Sugar: 5g; Protein: 5g; Fiber: 5g; Sodium: 44mg

GARLIC PARMESAN SMASHED BRUSSELS SPROUTS

Serves 4 / Prep time: 10 minutes / **Cook time:** 15 minutes

5 INGREDIENTS OR FEWER, QUICK

Brussels sprouts are a good source of fiber, B vitamins, and vitamin C. Smashing them before putting them in the oven gives the cooked Brussels sprouts a deliciously crispy crunch complemented perfectly by garlic and Parmesan cheese.

1 pound frozen Brussels
sprouts

1 tablespoon extra-virgin
olive oil

1 teaspoon garlic powder

¼ teaspoon salt

¼ teaspoon freshly ground
black pepper

¼ cup grated Parmesan
cheese, divided

1. Preheat the oven to 375°F.

2. Put the Brussels sprouts in a large microwave-safe bowl. Cover the bowl and microwave on high for 3 minutes, or until the Brussels sprouts are tender.

3. Add the oil, garlic powder, salt, pepper, and half of the Parmesan cheese and toss to coat.

4. Spread the seasoned Brussels sprouts evenly on two baking sheets, then press down on each one with the back of a wooden spoon to flatten them. Sprinkle the remaining Parmesan cheese over the sprouts.

5. Bake for 15 minutes, or until the Brussels sprouts are browned and crispy. Serve immediately.

INGREDIENT TIP: Don't overcrowd the baking sheets. Using two sheets gives the sprouts enough room to get crispy.

Per Serving: Calories: 107; Fat: 5g; Protein: 6g;
Carbohydrates: 12g; Fiber: 4g; Sugar: 3g; Sodium: 287mg

SMOKY PAPRIKA ROASTED POTATOES

Serves 4 / **Prep time:** 10 minutes / **Cook time:** 20 minutes

These roasted potatoes feature flavors inspired by ingredients commonly found in Spanish cuisine, and they are an easy, inexpensive way to bump up the flavor of the humble potato. They are great served with your favorite chicken or beef dish.

2 tablespoons tomato
  paste

2 tablespoons white
  vinegar

1 tablespoon extra-virgin
  olive oil

1½ teaspoons ground
  cumin

1½ teaspoons chili powder

1½ teaspoons smoked
  paprika

1½ pounds potatoes, diced

Salt

Freshly ground black
  pepper

1. Preheat the oven to 375°F.

2. In a large bowl, mix the tomato paste, vinegar, and oil.

3. Add the cumin, chili powder, and paprika, and stir to combine.

4. Add the potatoes to the bowl and stir to coat. Spread the potatoes evenly on two large baking sheets, and bake for 15 to 20 minutes, or until tender and crispy.

5. Season with salt and pepper to taste, then serve.

SHOPPING TIP: If you use potatoes frequently in your meals or recipes this week, go with the bagged option instead of loose potatoes for greater cost savings.

Per Serving: Calories: 176; Fat: 4g; Protein: 4g; Carbohydrates: 32g; Fiber: 3g; Sugar: 5g; Sodium: 85mg

WARM LENTIL SALAD

Serves 4 / **Prep time:** 10 minutes / **Cook time:** 10 minutes

DAIRY-FREE, QUICK, VEGETARIAN

This salad has lovely French-inspired flavors from the herbes de Provence and Dijon mustard. It can be served warm or at room temperature with just about any main dish. You can even make it an entrée by serving it on brown rice, mixed greens, or with grilled chicken.

3 tablespoons red wine vinegar

1½ tablespoons plus 1 teaspoon extra-virgin olive oil, divided

2 tablespoons Dijon mustard

2 teaspoons herbes de Provence

¼ teaspoon salt

¼ teaspoon freshly ground black pepper

1 large carrot, chopped

1 yellow onion, chopped

1 garlic clove, minced

2 (15-ounce) cans brown lentils, drained and rinsed

2 tablespoons chopped fresh parsley

1. In a small bowl, whisk the red wine vinegar, 1½ tablespoons olive oil, the mustard, the herbes de Provence, the salt, and the pepper until thoroughly combined, then set aside.

2. In a large skillet, heat the remaining 1 teaspoon of oil over medium heat.

3. Add the carrot, onion, and garlic to the skillet, and cook for 5 minutes, stirring occasionally until tender.

4. Once the vegetables are tender, add the lentils. Cook for an additional 2 minutes, or until the lentils are heated through.

5. Remove the skillet from the heat and stir in the dressing.

6. Transfer the salad to a serving dish and top with parsley before serving.

VARIATION TIP: Add a bit of heat by stirring in ¼ teaspoon of red pepper flakes before serving.

Per Serving: Calories: 250; Fat: 7g; Protein: 14g; Carbohydrates: 36g; Fiber: 14g; Sugar: 6g; Sodium: 117mg

SAVORY HUMMUS ENERGY BITES

Makes 12 bites / Prep time: 15 minutes

DAIRY-FREE, QUICK, VEGETARIAN

Energy bites aren't only made with dried fruit and nuts. This savory version is packed with flavor, as well as the fiber, protein, and healthy fats you need to fuel you through the afternoon slump—all in one bite!

2 cups rolled oats

¼ cup sunflower seeds

¼ cup pumpkin seeds

½ teaspoon Italian seasoning

¼ teaspoon salt

¼ teaspoon freshly ground black pepper

¼ teaspoon red pepper flakes

1 cup Quick Garlic Hummus (page 134), or store-bought hummus

1 tablespoon olive oil

1. In a large bowl, stir together the rolled oats, sunflower seeds, pumpkin seeds, Italian seasoning, salt, pepper, and red pepper flakes.

2. Add the hummus and oil and stir until combined.

3. Form the hummus mixture into 12 golf ball–size balls.

4. Refrigerate in an airtight container until ready to eat, or for up to 1 week.

SUBSTITUTION TIP: Changing up the flavor of these bites is as easy as changing up the flavor of the hummus you use; add roasted red pepper, chipotle, or garlic.

Per Serving (1 hummus bite): Calories: 138; Fat: 7g; Protein: 5g; Carbohydrates: 15g; Fiber: 3g; Sugar: 0g; Sodium: 105mg

HERBED FETA DIP WITH CUCUMBER SLICES

Serves 4 / **Prep time:** 10 minutes

5 INGREDIENTS OR FEWER, QUICK, VEGETARIAN

Everything is betta with feta, right? This feta dip is loaded with flavor and can be served up for easy entertaining or a quick midday snack. Feel free to replace the cucumbers with whichever vegetable is currently on sale or in season, or serve the dip with a mix of vegetables you have in your refrigerator.

6 ounces crumbled feta cheese

1 cup low-fat plain Greek yogurt

1 tablespoon plus 1 teaspoon extra-virgin olive oil

1 tablespoon freshly squeezed lemon juice

2 garlic cloves

½ teaspoon Italian seasoning

Freshly ground black pepper

1 large cucumber, sliced

1. In a blender or food processor, combine the feta, yogurt, lemon juice, garlic, Italian seasoning, and 1 tablespoon of oil. Blend on high for 1 minute, or until smooth.

2. Transfer the mixture to a serving bowl, sprinkle with pepper, and drizzle the remaining oil over the top.

3. Serve with cucumber slices.

SHOPPING TIP: Compare unit prices on blocks of feta cheese and crumbled varieties to see which is a better bargain. Often, the blocks are a more cost-effective option.

Per Serving (2 tablespoons of dip and 10 cucumber slices): Calories: 205; Fat: 15g; Protein: 10g; Carbohydrates: 10g; Fiber: 0g; Sugar: 7g; Sodium: 435mg

OVEN-BAKED PITA CHIPS

Serves 4 / Prep time: 5 minutes / **Cook time:** 10 minutes

5 INGREDIENTS OR FEWER, DAIRY-FREE, QUICK, VEGETARIAN

When you want something extra crispy for a midday snack, these pita chips fit the bill. Baking them in the oven not only gives them that quintessential crunch but is a healthier option than deep-fried chips or snacks. You can easily change the flavors by swapping out the seasonings for chili powder, cinnamon, or a little cayenne pepper.

3 (8-inch) whole wheat pita rounds

2 tablespoons extra-virgin olive oil

1½ teaspoons garlic powder

1 teaspoon Italian seasoning

1 teaspoon salt

1. Preheat the oven to 400°F.

2. Cut each pita into 8 equal wedges, and peel apart the layers to make 16 chips per pita round. Set aside.

3. In a large bowl, combine the oil, garlic powder, Italian seasoning, and salt and mix well.

4. Add the pita wedges to the bowl and toss until they are evenly coated.

5. Spread the pita out evenly on two large baking sheets, and bake for 8 to 10 minutes, or until the pita chips are golden brown and crispy.

VARIATION TIP: Want an extra-thick chip to hold all that hummus? Don't separate the layers when cutting, and bake for an extra few minutes until crispy.

Per Serving (12 pita chips): Calories: 213; Fat: 8g; Protein: 6g; Carbohydrates: 32g; Fiber: 4g; Sugar: 0g; Sodium: 831mg

BLUE CHEESE AND WALNUT STUFFED DATES

Serves 6 / Prep time: 15 minutes

5 INGREDIENTS OR FEWER, QUICK, VEGETARIAN

If you can't decide whether you want something sweet, salty, chewy, or crunchy, why not have them all? These stuffed dates satisfy any kind of snack you're craving. They are also an easy appetizer for guests.

18 pitted dates

3 ounces blue cheese

18 walnut halves

1. Slice each date down the middle (if not cut already), making sure not to go through the date all the way to keep the sides intact.

2. Stuff each date with blue cheese, followed by a walnut half, and serve immediately.

SUBSTITUTION TIP: Not big on blue cheese? Swap it out for goat cheese, ricotta, or Manchego.

Per Serving (3 stuffed dates): Calories: 147; Fat: 8g; Protein: 4g; Carbohydrates: 17g; Fiber: 2g; Sugar: 14g; Sodium: 163mg

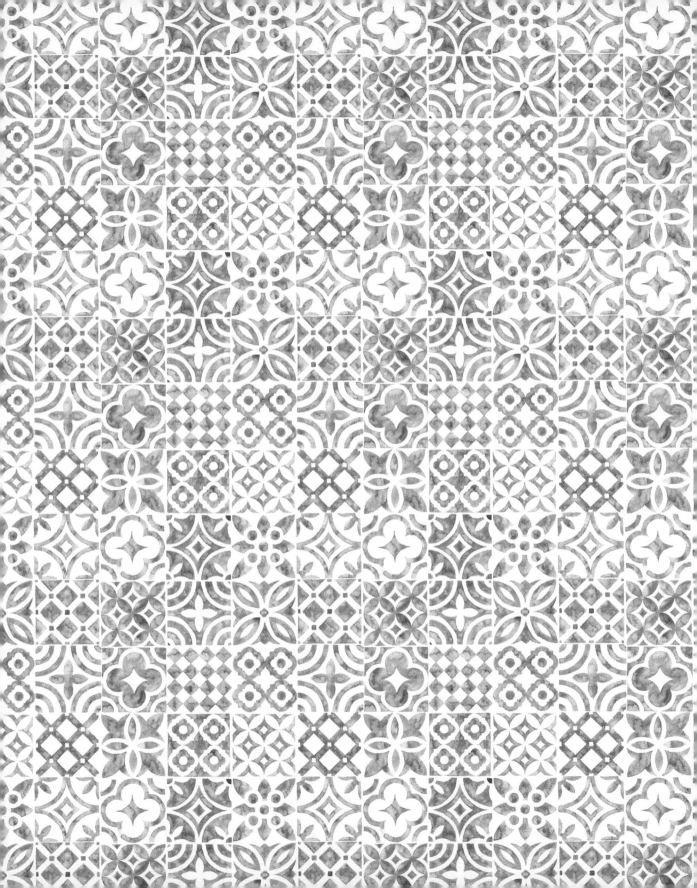

Lemon Orzo with Fresh Herbs, page 68

VEGETARIAN MAINS

JEWELED RICE

Serves 6 / **Prep time:** 15 minutes / **Cook time:** 30 minutes

Who needs diamonds when you can have jewel-studded rice instead? Okay, so they're not actually jewels, but it's the next best thing and a lot more edible. The vegetables and dried cranberries in this recipe inspired by chef Sanaa Abourezk not only give this dish a rich color but also help you load up on immune-supporting vitamins C and A.

¼ cup extra-virgin olive oil, divided

1 yellow onion, finely chopped

2 garlic cloves, minced

½ teaspoon peeled chopped fresh ginger

4½ cups water

¾ teaspoon salt, divided, plus more as needed

1 teaspoon ground turmeric

2 cups basmati rice

2 cups frozen peas and carrots

½ cup dried cranberries

Grated zest of 1 orange

⅛ teaspoon cayenne pepper

¼ cup sliced almonds, toasted

1. In a large pot, heat 2 tablespoons of oil over medium heat.

2. Add the onion and cook for 3 minutes, or until translucent. Add the garlic and ginger and cook for 1 minute.

3. Stir in the water, ½ teaspoon of salt, and the turmeric. Bring the mixture to a boil. Stir in the rice and return the mixture to a boil. Reduce the heat to low, cover the pot, and cook for 15 minutes. Turn off the heat. Let the rice rest on the burner, covered, for 5 minutes.

4. Meanwhile, in a medium skillet over medium-low heat, heat the remaining 2 tablespoons of oil. Stir in the peas and carrots, and cook for 2 minutes, or until softened.

5. Stir in the cranberries and orange zest. Season with the remaining ¼ teaspoon of salt and the cayenne pepper. Cook for 1 to 2 minutes.

6. Fluff the rice with a fork, and transfer to a serving platter. Top with the peas and carrots and a sprinkle of toasted almonds before serving.

INGREDIENT TIP: To toast almonds, add them to a skillet over low heat. Stir occasionally, until lightly browned and fragrant. Keep an eye on them to avoid burning.

Per Serving: Calories: 405; Fat: 12g; Protein: 7g; Carbohydrates: 68g; Fiber: 4g; Sugar: 10g; Sodium: 309mg

ROASTED CAULIFLOWER TAGINE

Serves 6 / Prep time: 15 minutes / **Cook time:** 35 minutes

DAIRY-FREE, ONE-POT, VEGETARIAN, WORTH THE WAIT

Referring to both the North African cooking vessel and the stew-like dish often cooked inside it, tagines are popular in Moroccan cuisine. This version inspired by chef Sanaa Abourezk isn't cooked in a tagine, but it still has a unique depth of flavor, and can be served on its own or with cooked brown rice or couscous.

2 tablespoons extra-virgin olive oil

1 large onion, chopped

4 garlic cloves, thinly sliced

2 cauliflower heads, cut into florets

6 cups water

1 (28-ounce) can low-sodium diced tomatoes

1 tablespoon tomato paste

1 teaspoon ground coriander

½ teaspoon salt

2 large russet potatoes, peeled and cut into 1-inch cubes

1 (15-ounce) can chickpeas, drained and rinsed

½ cup chopped fresh cilantro

2 tablespoons freshly squeezed lemon juice

1 teaspoon grated lemon zest

1. In a large pot, heat the oil over medium heat. Add the onion and sauté for 2 to 3 minutes, or until browned.

2. Stir in the garlic and cook for an additional 30 seconds. Add the cauliflower and cook for 5 minutes or until browned.

3. Stir in the water, tomatoes, tomato paste, coriander, and salt until well combined. Increase the heat to high and bring it to a boil.

4. Stir in the potatoes, then bring the mixture back to a boil. Reduce the heat to medium and cook for about 10 minutes until the potatoes are fork-tender but not mushy.

5. Add the chickpeas, and simmer over low heat for 10 minutes to warm through. Before serving, stir in the cilantro, lemon juice, and lemon zest.

SUBSTITUTION TIP: You can also use frozen cauliflower instead of fresh. Just add 8 cups of frozen cauliflower with the potatoes.

Per Serving: Calories: 331; Fat: 7g; Protein: 13g; Carbohydrates: 58g; Fiber: 13g; Sugar: 11g; Sodium: 249mg

LEMON ORZO WITH FRESH HERBS

Serves 4 / Prep time: 10 minutes / **Cook time:** 10 minutes

5 INGREDIENTS OR FEWER, DAIRY-FREE, QUICK, VEGETARIAN

Whether it's dusk on a warm summer night or in the dead of winter, this bright and flavorful pasta dish inspired by cookbook author Denise Hazime will add a pop of freshness to your dinner table. The flavor is even better the next day, so enjoy it for dinner the first night and have delicious leftovers for lunch.

2 cups orzo

½ cup extra-virgin olive oil

⅓ cup freshly squeezed
   lemon juice

1 teaspoon salt

½ teaspoon freshly ground
   black pepper

1 cup grape tomatoes,
   halved

½ cup finely chopped fresh
   parsley

½ cup finely chopped fresh
   basil

2 tablespoons grated
   lemon zest

1. Bring a large pot of water to a boil. Add the orzo and cook for 7 minutes, or until al dente. Drain the pasta and rinse it with cold water. Let the orzo sit in a strainer to cool slightly (it should still be a bit warm).

2. While the pasta is cooling, in a large bowl, whisk together the oil, lemon juice, salt, and pepper.

3. Transfer the orzo to the bowl and add the tomatoes, parsley, basil, and lemon zest.

4. Toss until the pasta is fully coated, then season with additional salt and pepper, if needed.

5. Serve at room temperature or chilled.

VARIATION TIP: For a little extra protein, add a can of rinsed chickpeas or cannellini beans, or add some crumbled feta for added flavor.

Per Serving: Calories: 578; Fat: 28g; Protein: 12g; Carbohydrates: 70g; Fiber: 5g; Sugar: 2g; Sodium: 597mg

ROASTED RED PEPPER AND GOAT CHEESE CHICKPEA BURGERS

Serves 4 / Prep time: 10 minutes / **Cook time:** 10 minutes

QUICK, VEGETARIAN

If you ask me, you can't go wrong with roasted red peppers and goat cheese, especially when mixed into this masterpiece of a bean burger. Chickpeas add plenty of plant-based protein and fiber to these burgers.

1 (28-ounce) can chickpeas, drained and rinsed

1 garlic clove, minced

2 tablespoons whole wheat flour

¼ teaspoon salt

½ cup diced roasted red peppers

2 ounces (¼ cup) crumbled goat cheese

2 teaspoons extra-virgin olive oil

4 whole wheat hamburger buns

1 batch Balsamic Caramelized Onions (page 139)

1 cup arugula

1. In a large bowl, combine the chickpeas, garlic, flour, and salt. Using a potato masher or a large fork, mash until most chickpeas are crushed.

2. Stir in the roasted red peppers and goat cheese. Using clean hands, form the mixture into 4 patties.

3. In a large skillet, heat the oil over medium heat. Place the burger patties into the skillet, and cook for 3 to 4 minutes per side, or until browned and crispy.

4. Transfer each patty to a hamburger bun, and top with the caramelized onions and arugula before serving.

INGREDIENT TIP: If the mixture seems too wet, add an extra tablespoon of flour. If it is too dry, add a tablespoon or two of water.

Per Serving (1 chickpea burger with toppings): Calories: 415; Fat: 11g; Protein: 19g; Carbohydrates: 65g; Fiber: 14g; Sugar: 13g; Sodium: 447mg

SMASHED LENTIL SALAD WITH AVOCADO AND FETA

Serves 4 / Prep time: 15 minutes

ONE-POT, QUICK, VEGETARIAN

Lentils are one of my favorite legumes because of their versatility, and they are a nutrition powerhouse. They are full of fiber, protein, folate, vitamin B_6, and iron, an important nutrient for energy and immunity. Try serving this salad sandwich style or even on a bed of mixed greens.

2 (15-ounce) cans brown lentils, drained and rinsed

2 tablespoons Quick Garlic Hummus (page 134), or store-bought hummus

2 tablespoons freshly squeezed lemon juice

½ tablespoon Dijon mustard

1 garlic clove, minced

½ teaspoon salt

½ avocado, cubed

¼ cup chopped red onion (about ½ small)

½ cup chopped carrot (about 1 medium)

¼ cup crumbled feta cheese

¼ cup chopped parsley

1. In a large bowl, use a potato masher or the back of a fork to mash the lentils, leaving a few lentils intact.

2. Add the hummus, lemon juice, mustard, garlic, and salt. Stir to combine. If the mixture is too dry, add 1 or 2 tablespoons of hummus.

3. Stir in the avocado, red onion, carrot, feta, and parsley, and serve.

VARIATION TIP: Don't have lentils? This salad can be made with chickpeas, cannellini beans, or white beans instead.

Per Serving: Calories: 266; Fat: 7g; Protein: 16g; Carbohydrates: 38g; Fiber: 15g; Sugar: 5g; Sodium: 435mg

MOROCCAN-INSPIRED TOFU QUINOA BOWLS

Serves 4 / **Prep time:** 10 minutes / **Cook time:** 20 minutes

DAIRY-FREE, QUICK, VEGETARIAN

These quinoa bowls are inspired by ingredients commonly found in Moroccan cuisine, such as dried apricots, almonds, and turmeric, which bring the perfect balance of sweet, earthy, tender, and crunchy to the dish. Couscous is used most frequently in Moroccan cooking, but I replaced it with quinoa to bump up the protein and fiber in this recipe.

¼ cup plus 2 teaspoons extra-virgin olive oil, divided

1 (12-ounce) block firm tofu, drained and cubed

3 tablespoons orange juice

1 tablespoon honey

½ teaspoon salt

½ teaspoon turmeric

½ teaspoon ground cumin

¼ teaspoon ground cinnamon

2 cups Super-Fluffy Quinoa (page 141)

⅓ cup sliced almonds

⅓ cup chopped dried apricots

½ cup chopped parsley

1. In a large skillet, heat 2 teaspoons of oil over medium heat. Add the tofu and cook until the tofu has browned. Cook in two batches if needed to avoid overcrowding the skillet.

2. In a large bowl, combine the remaining ¼ cup of oil with the orange juice, honey, salt, turmeric, cumin, and cinnamon, and mix well. Add the cooked quinoa and stir to combine.

3. Divide the quinoa mixture evenly between 4 bowls, and top each serving with equal amounts of tofu, almonds, apricots, and parsley.

INGREDIENT TIP: Look for tofu in your grocery store's produce section. Before cooking, wrap the block of tofu in a kitchen towel, place it on a plate or cutting board, and press it with a heavy skillet to get the excess water out.

Per Serving: Calories: 430; Fat: 26g; Protein: 18g; Carbohydrates: 37g; Fiber: 5g; Sugar: 13g; Sodium: 312mg

PAPRIKA TOFU

Serves 4 / **Prep time:** 10 minutes / **Cook time:** 20 minutes

DAIRY-FREE, ONE-POT, QUICK, VEGETARIAN

This dish is a variation on the Hungarian dish chicken paprikash, which comes from the paprika used to flavor it. Thanks to tofu and light coconut milk, this vegetarian version has the same wonderful flavor but less fat and more fiber. Enjoy this dish with a side of brown rice, quinoa, or whole-grain pita bread.

1 tablespoon extra-virgin olive oil

1 (12-ounce) container extra-firm tofu, drained and cubed

1 small yellow onion, chopped

2 garlic cloves, minced

1 tomato, chopped

1 red bell pepper, seeded and chopped

½ cup light coconut milk

2 tablespoons whole wheat flour

1½ cups low-sodium vegetable broth

1 tablespoon sweet paprika

½ teaspoon salt

¼ teaspoon cayenne pepper

1. In a large skillet, heat the oil over medium-high heat.

2. Add the tofu, and cook for 5 minutes, or until browned. Remove the tofu from the skillet with a slotted spoon and set it aside.

3. Put the onion, garlic, tomato, and bell pepper into the same skillet, and cook for 3 minutes, or until the onion and pepper have softened.

4. In a small bowl, whisk together the coconut milk and flour. Set aside.

5. Add the vegetable broth, paprika, salt, and cayenne pepper to the skillet.

6. Whisk the coconut milk mixture into the ingredients in the skillet, then whisk constantly while bringing the liquid to a boil.

7. Continue cooking for 3 to 5 minutes, or until the sauce is thickened. Add the tofu, then reduce the heat to medium-low and simmer for 5 minutes before removing the pan from the heat. Serve immediately.

VARIATION TIP: If you want to increase the spicy and smoky flavor, use 2 teaspoons of sweet paprika and 1 teaspoon of smoked paprika. You can also increase the amount of cayenne pepper for an added kick.

Per Serving: Calories: 178; Fat: 12g; Protein: 10g; Carbohydrates: 11g; Fiber: 2g; Sugar: 3g; Sodium: 304mg

ARTICHOKE AND RED ONION FLATBREAD WITH RICOTTA

Serves 4 / Prep time: 5 minutes / **Cook time:** 10 minutes

ONE-POT, QUICK

Fridays and pizza go together like . . . Fridays and pizza! But these flatbreads are so quick and easy to make, you don't have to wait until Friday to enjoy them. This recipe can be scaled up or down to serve a crowd or a party of one.

4 (8-inch) whole wheat pita rounds

1½ cups part-skim shredded mozzarella cheese

3 garlic cloves, minced

¼ cup grated Parmesan cheese

1 cup canned quartered artichoke hearts, drained

½ small red onion, thinly sliced

½ cup part-skim ricotta cheese

1 tablespoon extra-virgin olive oil

1. Preheat the oven to 375°F.

2. Place the pita rounds on one or two large baking sheets. Top each pita with mozzarella cheese, garlic, Parmesan cheese, artichokes, and onion.

3. Drop 2 dollops (about 1 tablespoon each) of ricotta cheese on top of each pita and transfer the baking sheets to the oven.

4. Bake for 8 to 10 minutes, or until the cheese is melted and the bottoms are golden brown. Drizzle each pita with oil before serving.

VARIATION TIP: Add a sweet element to your flatbread by adding dried cranberries or thinly sliced pears before baking.

INGREDIENT TIP: Most Parmesan cheeses use animal rennet, so if you're strictly vegetarian or vegan, look for Parmesan without rennet.

Per Serving (1 flatbread): Calories: 403; Fat: 16g; Protein: 23g; Carbohydrates: 44g; Fiber: 7g; Sugar: 2g; Sodium: 614mg

KALE AND NAVY BEAN STEW

Serves 6 / **Prep time:** 10 minutes / **Cook time:** 15 minutes

DAIRY-FREE, ONE-POT, QUICK, VEGETARIAN

Nothing is more satisfying than a thick and hearty stew on a chilly or rainy day. This quick-cooking stew uses mashed beans to give it more body and thickness that pairs perfectly with a hearty green like kale. Serve it with a hunk of crusty whole-grain bread for dipping.

1 tablespoon extra-virgin olive oil

1 large yellow onion, diced

3 garlic cloves, minced

2 medium carrots, diced

2 (15-ounce) cans navy beans, drained and rinsed, divided

1 (28-ounce) can low-sodium diced tomatoes

3 cups low-sodium vegetable broth

1 teaspoon salt

1 teaspoon dried oregano

4 cups chopped kale (1 bunch)

1. In a large pot, heat the oil over medium-high heat.

2. Add the onion, garlic, and carrots, and sauté for 5 minutes, or until the vegetables start to soften.

3. In a small bowl, mash 1 cup of navy beans with a potato masher or fork to form a paste.

4. Add the mashed beans, the remaining navy beans, the tomatoes, the vegetable broth, the salt, and the oregano to the pot, and bring the liquid to a boil.

5. Reduce the heat to low, add the kale, and simmer for 2 to 3 minutes, or until the kale has started to wilt and soften. Remove from the heat and serve.

INGREDIENT TIP: Look for prewashed and chopped kale at your grocery store. It saves time and effort and is not much more expensive.

Per Serving: Calories: 195; Fat: 3g; Protein: 10g; Carbohydrates: 34g; Fiber: 14g; Sugar: 6g; Sodium: 420mg

ARUGULA AND CANNELLINI BEAN POLENTA

Serves 4 / Prep time: 10 minutes / **Cook time:** 15 minutes

DAIRY-FREE, QUICK, VEGETARIAN

Polenta is a common ingredient in Italian cooking, sometimes referred to as "Italian grits." Making it creamy and flavorful doesn't have to include tons of butter and cheese, especially when topped with this flavorful sauce of cannellini beans and peppery arugula. Using quick-cooking polenta means you can pull this meal together in less than 30 minutes.

1 tablespoon extra-virgin
  olive oil, divided
1 yellow onion, diced
3 garlic cloves, minced
1 (28-ounce) can cannellini
  beans, drained and rinsed
4 cups low-sodium
  vegetable broth, divided
1 teaspoon dried oregano
6 cups arugula
2 teaspoons red wine
  vinegar
1 cup quick-cooking
  polenta
½ teaspoon salt

1. In a large sauté pan, heat ½ tablespoon of oil over medium-high heat. Add the onion, and cook for 3 to 4 minutes, or until softened.

2. Add the garlic and cook for an additional 30 seconds before stirring in the beans, 1 cup of vegetable broth, and the oregano.

3. Cover and bring the mixture to a boil. Then reduce the heat to low and simmer for 4 minutes.

4. Stir in the arugula and red wine vinegar and continue cooking until the arugula has wilted. Keep warm over low heat while preparing the polenta.

5. In a large saucepan, bring the remaining 3 cups of vegetable broth to a boil over high heat.

6. Whisk in the polenta, reduce the heat to low, and continue cooking for 5 to 6 minutes, stirring often, until the polenta has thickened. Stir in the remaining ½ tablespoon of oil and salt then divide evenly between four bowls. Top each bowl with bean mixture before serving.

VARIATION TIP: Replace the arugula with your favorite greens, such as baby spinach, chopped kale, or chopped Swiss chard.

Per Serving: Calories: 382; Fat: 5g; Protein: 15g;
Carbohydrates: 69g; Fiber: 17g; Sugar: 3g; Sodium: 991mg

SPANAKOPITA LASAGNA

Serves 6 / **Prep time:** 10 minutes / **Cook time:** 50 minutes, plus 5 minutes to rest

WORTH THE WAIT

Spanakopita is a Greek pastry dish usually made with flaky phyllo dough, salty feta cheese, and lots of spinach. In this recipe, I've turned it into a hearty lasagna that is fit to feed a crowd and full of the same rich flavor and nourishing fillings.

1 (13-ounce) package whole wheat lasagna noodles

1 tablespoon extra-virgin olive oil, divided

1 yellow onion, diced

3 garlic cloves, minced

1 teaspoon dried dill

1 (16-ounce) bag frozen chopped spinach, thawed and thoroughly drained

6 ounces (1½ cups) crumbled feta cheese

¼ cup chopped fresh parsley

3 cups part-skim ricotta cheese

3 large eggs

¼ cup plus 2 tablespoons grated Parmesan cheese

¼ teaspoon ground nutmeg (optional)

⅓ cup part-skim mozzarella cheese

1. Cook the lasagna noodles according to the package instructions. Drain and toss with ½ tablespoon of oil to prevent sticking. Set them aside.

2. Preheat the oven to 375°F. Lightly coat a 9-by-13-inch pan with the remaining oil and set aside.

3. In a large bowl, mix the onion, garlic, dill, spinach, feta, and parsley until well combined.

4. In a separate bowl, mix the ricotta cheese, eggs, ¼ cup of Parmesan cheese, and nutmeg (if using).

5. Spread one-third of the ricotta mixture into the prepared pan in an even layer, then cover it with a layer of lasagna noodles. Top the noodles with half the spinach mixture and spread it in an even layer. Starting with the ricotta, repeat the process one more time.

6. Top with one more layer of lasagna noodles, spread the remaining third of the ricotta mixture over the noodles, and sprinkle the mozzarella cheese and remaining Parmesan cheese over the top.

7. Cover the lasagna with aluminum foil and bake for 30 minutes. Remove the foil, and bake for another 10 minutes, or until the cheese has melted.

8. Let the lasagna cool for 5 minutes before slicing and serving.

INGREDIENT TIP: Most Parmesan cheeses use animal rennet, so if you're strictly vegetarian or vegan, look for Parmesan without rennet.

Per Serving: Calories: 585; Fat: 25g; Protein: 38g; Carbohydrates: 59g; Fiber: 7g; Sugar: 3g; Sodium: 583mg

ONE-POT RICE AND BEANS

Serves 6 / **Prep time:** 10 minutes / **Cook time:** 40 minutes

DAIRY-FREE, ONE-POT, VEGETARIAN, WORTH THE WAIT

The pairing of rice and beans is a long-standing staple in multiple cultures, especially in many Latin American and African countries such as Brazil and Ghana. This dish gives you a lot of bang for your buck, because it is inexpensive to prepare but deliciously satisfying and hearty. Make it ahead of time and enjoy it throughout the week.

1 tablespoon extra-virgin olive oil, divided

1 yellow onion, diced

3 garlic cloves, minced

1 teaspoon chili powder

1 teaspoon smoked paprika

1 teaspoon ground cumin

1 teaspoon salt

1 (15-ounce) can fire-roasted diced tomatoes

2 cups brown rice

3 cups low-sodium vegetable broth

1 (28-ounce) can kidney beans, drained and rinsed

½ cup chopped cilantro

1. In a large pot, heat the oil over medium-high heat. Stir in the onion, and sauté for 3 minutes, or until softened. Add the garlic and cook for another 30 seconds.

2. Add the chili powder, paprika, cumin, and salt, and cook for 30 seconds. Stir in the tomatoes, rice, and broth, and bring the liquid to a boil.

3. Reduce the heat to medium-low, cover, and simmer for 35 to 40 minutes, or until the rice is tender.

4. Stir in the beans and remove the pot from the heat. Season with additional salt or spices, as needed.

5. Top with chopped cilantro and serve.

VARIATION TIP: If you don't have kidney beans on hand, make this dish with black beans or red beans.

Per Serving: Calories: 386; Fat: 5g; Protein: 13g; Carbohydrates: 73g; Fiber: 10g; Sugar: 4g; Sodium: 488mg

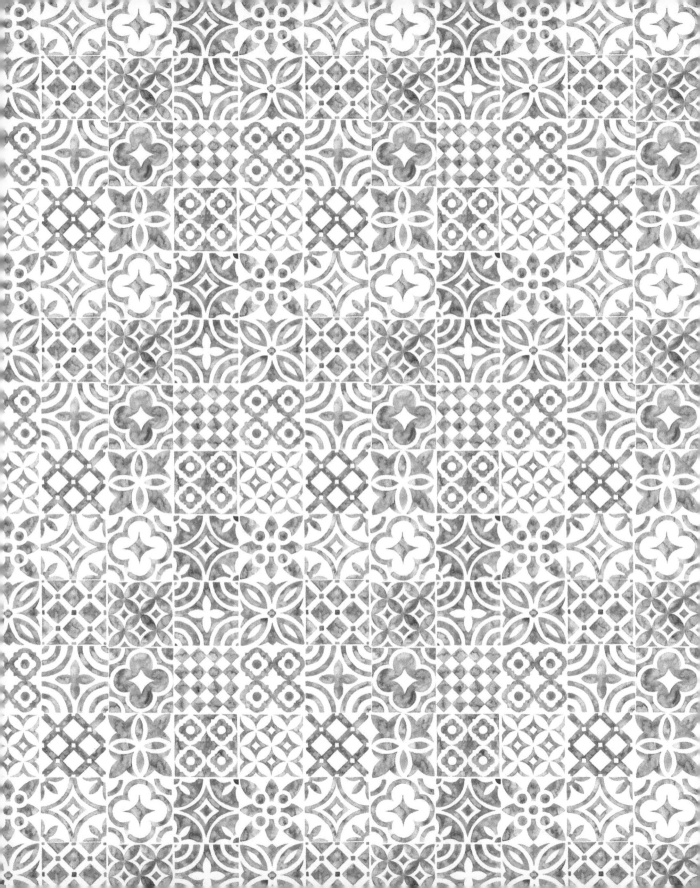

Salmon Provençal, **page 84**

SEAFOOD & FISH

WHITEFISH WITH LEMON AND CAPERS

Serves 4 / **Prep time:** 5 minutes / **Cook time:** 20 minutes

5 INGREDIENTS OR FEWER, QUICK

This delicate whitefish recipe inspired by cookbook author Denise Hazime is simple to prepare, but that doesn't mean it doesn't pack some serious flavor. The bright and briny caper sauce is an easy way to add flavor, and you can swap in any seafood, including scallops, shrimp, or salmon. Serve with roasted vegetables, brown rice, or a simple green salad.

4 (5-ounce) cod fillets (or any whitefish)

2 tablespoons extra-virgin olive oil, divided

1 teaspoon salt, divided

1 tablespoon unsalted butter

2 tablespoons capers, drained

3 tablespoons freshly squeezed lemon juice

½ teaspoon freshly ground black pepper

1. Preheat the oven to 450°F. Line a 9-by-13-inch baking dish with aluminum foil.

2. Place the cod in the baking dish and pat it dry with a paper towel. Drizzle 1 tablespoon of oil over the fish and season with ½ teaspoon of salt.

3. Bake for 15 minutes, or until the fish is opaque and flakes easily with a fork.

4. Make the caper sauce in the last few minutes of baking the fish. In a small saucepan, melt the butter with the remaining tablespoon of oil over medium heat. Add the capers, the lemon juice, the remaining ½ teaspoon of salt, and the black pepper. Simmer the sauce for 30 seconds or until warmed through.

5. Transfer the baked fish to a serving dish and spoon the caper sauce over each portion before serving.

VARIATION TIP: Add 1 teaspoon of grated lemon zest to the sauce while cooking for extra fresh lemon flavor. You can also sprinkle the fish with chopped parsley or dill for a pop of color and flavor.

Per Serving (1 cod fillet with lemon and caper sauce):
Calories: 205; Fat: 11g; Protein: 25g; Carbohydrates: 1g; Fiber: 0g; Sugar: 0g; Sodium: 760mg

SALMON PROVENÇAL

Serves 4 / Prep time: 15 minutes / **Cook time:** 25 minutes

DAIRY-FREE, ONE-POT

Provençal cuisine, originating from the Provence region of France, uses seasonal produce, a warm climate, and native ingredients. No matter where in the world you are making this dish, inspired by dietitian Susan Zogheib, the first bite will instantly bring you to the southeast of France. Salmon is rich in muscle-building protein, heart-healthy omega-3 fats, and essential vitamins and minerals.

1 tablespoon extra-virgin olive oil

1 red bell pepper, seeded and chopped

1 small yellow onion, chopped

3 garlic cloves, minced

3 large tomatoes, chopped

2 cups shredded kale

¼ cup dry white wine

¼ cup sliced black olives

2 tablespoons capers

2 teaspoons chopped fresh thyme

2 teaspoons chopped fresh parsley

4 (4-ounce) salmon fillets

1. Preheat the oven to 400°F.

2. In a large ovenproof skillet, heat the oil over medium-high heat. Sauté the bell pepper, onion, and garlic for 3 to 4 minutes, or until softened.

3. Add the tomatoes, kale, and wine, and bring the mixture to a boil. Reduce the heat to low, and simmer for 5 minutes, or until the sauce thickens slightly.

4. Stir in the olives, capers, thyme, and parsley. Add the salmon fillets to the sauce, cover the skillet, and bake in the oven for 15 to 20 minutes, or until the fish flakes easily with a fork.

5. Remove from the oven and transfer the salmon to a serving dish. Spoon the sauce over the salmon before serving.

SUBSTITUTION TIP: If you don't have white wine, you can replace it with chicken or vegetable stock.

Per Serving (1 salmon fillet with sauce): Calories: 263; Fat: 12g; Protein: 25g; Carbohydrates: 11g; Fiber: 3g; Sugar: 6g; Sodium: 246mg

OPEN-FACED CAPRESE TUNA MELTS

Serves 4 / Prep time: 5 minutes / **Cook time:** 10 minutes

ONE-POT, QUICK

Named after the island of Capri in Italy, Caprese is a simple salad made from fresh tomatoes, basil, and mozzarella. This twist on the Mediterranean classic combines the flavors of a Caprese salad with budget-friendly canned tuna to create a delicious and healthy sandwich.

2 (5-ounce) cans chunk white tuna, drained

1 tablespoon extra-virgin olive oil

1 garlic clove, minced

1 teaspoon Italian seasoning

Nonstick cooking spray

4 slices whole-grain bread

1 large tomato, sliced

16 fresh basil leaves

6 ounces sliced fresh mozzarella

1 tablespoon Balsamic Glaze (page 138) (optional)

1. In a medium bowl, mix the tuna, oil, garlic, and Italian seasoning.

2. Heat a large skillet over medium-low heat and coat with nonstick cooking spray. Place two slices of bread into the skillet and top each slice with one-quarter of the sliced tomatoes, one-quarter of the tuna mixture, four basil leaves, and one-quarter of the sliced mozzarella cheese.

3. Cover the pan, and cook for 3 to 4 minutes, or until the cheese has melted and the bread is crispy. Repeat with the remaining two slices of bread and ingredients.

4. Drizzle each sandwich with Balsamic Glaze (if using) before serving.

VARIATION TIP: You can also make this dish with boneless, skinless canned salmon or canned mackerel.

Per Serving (1 open-faced sandwich): Calories: 304; Fat: 16g; Protein: 26g; Carbohydrates: 13g; Fiber: 2g; Sugar: 3g; Sodium: 581mg

PESTO-CRUSTED SALMON WITH BROILED TOMATOES

Serves 4 / Prep time: 10 minutes / **Cook time:** 20 minutes

5 INGREDIENTS OR FEWER, ONE-POT, QUICK

Using a higher heat to cook salmon gives it a crispy exterior texture while keeping it tender and juicy on the inside. The pesto adds a burst of bright flavor at first bite while locking in the moisture even further. Pair this with your favorite roasted vegetables, such as Skillet Asparagus with Lemon Zest and Red Pepper Flakes (page 52).

4 (5-ounce) salmon fillets (fresh or frozen and thawed)

1 batch Walnut Basil Pesto (page 132)

4 Roma tomatoes, sliced

1. Preheat the oven to 400°F. Line a baking sheet with aluminum foil or parchment paper.

2. Place the salmon fillets on the baking sheet and coat each with pesto.

3. Layer the tomatoes on top of the pesto to cover each salmon fillet.

4. Bake for 15 to 20 minutes, or until the fish flakes easily with a fork.

INGREDIENT TIP: Short on time? Buy your favorite jarred pesto instead, or make basil pesto ahead of time, and refrigerate in a sealed container for up to 3 days.

Per Serving (1 salmon fillet with pesto): Calories: 384; Fat: 27g; Protein: 32g; Carbohydrates: 4g; Fiber: 1g; Sugar: 2g; Sodium: 354mg

SALAD NIÇOISE WITH MACKEREL

Serves 4 / **Prep time:** 10 minutes / **Cook time:** 20 minutes

DAIRY-FREE, ONE-POT, QUICK

Named after the city of Nice in France, the Niçoise salad uses affordable ingredients such as canned fish, potatoes, and eggs to make a filling and nutritious salad. In this version, I swapped out the typical tuna for mackerel, which has a taste and texture similar to tuna, but has a higher amount of heart-healthy omega-3 fatty acids. Boil your eggs and potatoes ahead of time to make this dish even quicker to prepare.

4 large eggs

1 pound red-skinned potatoes, thickly sliced

1 head romaine lettuce, chopped

1 cup cherry tomatoes, halved

1 (12-ounce) bag frozen cut green beans, thawed and drained

½ cup pitted kalamata olives

2 (5-ounce) cans boneless, skinless mackerel, drained and flaked

1 batch Simple French Vinaigrette (page 137)

1. In a medium pot, bring sufficient water to cover the eggs to a boil. Carefully add the eggs to the boiling water and cook for 7 minutes for a jammy yolk or 9 minutes for a firm yolk. Using a slotted spoon, transfer the eggs to a bowl of ice water. Let cool for 5 minutes before peeling. Slice each egg in half and set them aside.

2. In the same pot, bring fresh water to a boil and carefully slip in the potatoes. Cook for 5 minutes, or until fork-tender but not mushy. Drain and let cool.

3. Divide the romaine evenly between four dinner plates. Top each with one-quarter of the cherry tomatoes, green beans, boiled potatoes, olives, and mackerel.

4. Put two halves of the eggs on the salad. Drizzle the dressing over each salad just before serving.

SHOPPING TIP: You can find canned mackerel in the same aisle as canned tuna at most grocery stores or supermarkets. Generally, canned mackerel is only $1 more than tuna, which equals 50 cents more per serving.

Per Serving: Calories: 396; Fat: 17g; Protein: 26g; Carbohydrates: 36g; Fiber: 8g; Sugar: 10g; Sodium: 738mg

SCALLOP SCAMPI WITH CRISPY SHALLOTS

Serves 4 / Prep time: 10 minutes / **Cook time:** 25 minutes

This simple pasta dish is made with smaller bay scallops, which tend to be more affordable than sea scallops, but with the same flavor and texture you know and love. Using a combination of olive oil and butter provides a luxurious flavor, but also helps lower the amount of saturated fat and adds more heart-friendly unsaturated fats in the process. I love the extra crunch of the crispy shallot topping in this dish.

1 pound whole wheat linguine

3 tablespoons extra-virgin olive oil, divided

1 tablespoon unsalted butter

4 garlic cloves, minced

1 pound bay scallops

1 teaspoon salt

½ teaspoon red pepper flakes

¼ cup low-sodium chicken broth

Juice and grated zest of 1 lemon

1 large shallot, thinly sliced

½ cup chopped fresh flat-leaf parsley

2 tablespoons grated Parmesan cheese (optional)

1. Cook the linguine according to package instructions. (After the noodles are cooked, drain them and set aside.)

2. While the linguine is cooking, in a large skillet or sauté pan over medium heat, heat 1 tablespoon of oil and 1 tablespoon of butter. Add the garlic and cook for 30 seconds, or until fragrant.

3. Add the scallops, salt, and red pepper flakes, and cook for 6 to 8 minutes, or until the scallops are opaque and cooked through.

4. Stir in the chicken broth, lemon juice, and lemon zest, and cook for another minute before removing the pan from the heat.

5. In a small skillet, heat the remaining 2 tablespoons of oil over medium heat. Add the shallot and cook for 5 minutes, or until golden brown.

6. Divide the linguine between 4 serving bowls, then top with one-quarter of the scallops. Sprinkle the parsley, Parmesan cheese (if using), and shallot over each serving.

SUBSTITUTION TIP: Dry white wine can be used in place of the chicken broth if desired. The linguine can also be swapped for your favorite whole wheat long pasta, such as angel-hair pasta or spaghetti.

Per Serving: Calories: 599; Fat: 15g; Protein: 31g; Carbohydrates: 91g; Fiber: 10g; Sugar: 1g; Sodium: 941mg

SPICY TOMATO SHRIMP OVER POLENTA

Serves 4 / Prep time: 10 minutes / **Cook time:** 15 minutes

DAIRY-FREE, QUICK

If you've ever had shrimp and grits, you'll know where I got my inspiration for this dish. This Mediterranean-inspired spin on the classic features creamy polenta, lots of garlic, and heart-healthy fats from olive oil instead of butter. If you like more of a kick, simply bump up the amount of red pepper flakes or cayenne pepper to your liking.

2 tablespoons extra-virgin olive oil, divided

1 yellow onion, chopped

3 garlic cloves, minced

1½ pounds shrimp, peeled, deveined, and tails removed

3½ cups low-sodium chicken broth, divided

1 (14-ounce) can low-sodium diced tomatoes

1 teaspoon smoked paprika

½ teaspoon red pepper flakes

⅛ teaspoon cayenne pepper

1 cup quick-cooking polenta

½ teaspoon salt

1. In a large skillet or sauté pan, heat 1 tablespoon of oil over medium heat.

2. Add the onion and cook for 3 minutes, or until softened. Add the garlic, and cook for an additional 30 seconds, or until fragrant.

3. Add the shrimp, ½ cup of chicken broth, the tomatoes, the paprika, the red pepper flakes, and the cayenne pepper, reduce the heat to low, and simmer for 8 minutes.

4. While the shrimp is cooking, make the polenta. In a large saucepan, bring the remaining 3 cups of chicken broth to a boil over high heat.

5. Whisk in the polenta once it is boiling and reduce heat to medium-low. Continue cooking for 5 minutes, stirring frequently until the polenta has thickened.

6. Season the polenta with salt and the remaining table-spoon of oil. Divide the polenta between four bowls.

7. Remove the shrimp from the heat and spoon them over the polenta before serving.

VARIATION TIP: The shrimp can also be served over brown rice, whole wheat pasta, or quinoa instead of polenta.

Per Serving: Calories: 375; Fat: 9g; Protein: 38g; Carbohydrates: 37g; Fiber: 4g; Sugar: 4g; Sodium: 905mg

SALMON PATTIES WITH DILL YOGURT SAUCE

Serves 4 / **Prep time:** 15 minutes / **Cook time:** 10 minutes

ONE-POT, QUICK

Canned fish is a quick, easy, and affordable way to prepare and enjoy more seafood. This recipe primarily uses pantry staples, making it perfect for a busy weeknight. You can serve these salmon patties on whole wheat hamburger buns, over a green salad, or on their own with your favorite sides.

FOR THE PATTIES

3 (5-ounce) cans boneless, skinless salmon, drained

3 large eggs

⅓ cup Italian bread crumbs

⅓ cup chopped fresh parsley

1 tablespoon Dijon mustard

1 tablespoon freshly squeezed lemon juice

2 teaspoons garlic powder

1 tablespoon extra-virgin olive oil

FOR THE SAUCE

½ cup low-fat plain Greek yogurt

1 teaspoon dried dill

1 teaspoon garlic powder

2 teaspoons extra-virgin olive oil

1. **To make the patties:** In a large bowl, mix the salmon, eggs, bread crumbs, parsley, mustard, lemon juice, and garlic powder until well combined.

2. Using clean hands, form the salmon mixture into four patties and refrigerate for 10 minutes.

3. **To make the sauce:** In a medium bowl, mix the yogurt, dill, garlic powder, and oil. Set aside.

4. In a large skillet, heat 1 tablespoon of oil over medium heat and cook the salmon patties for 3 to 4 minutes per side, or until golden brown and crispy.

5. Top each patty with yogurt sauce before serving.

VARIATION TIP: Add a bit of salty flavor by adding a tablespoon or two of capers or chopped black olives to the patties in step 1 before cooking.

Per Serving (1 salmon patty with dill yogurt sauce):
Calories: 312; Fat: 16g; Protein: 28g; Carbohydrates: 15g; Fiber: 1g; Sugar: 3g; Sodium: 548mg

MUSSELS PUTTANESCA WITH SPAGHETTI

Serves 4 / **Prep time:** 5 minutes / **Cook time:** 25 minutes

DAIRY-FREE, QUICK

The secret to a good homemade sauce is the simmer. Cooking this tomato sauce low and slow gives it a deeper, richer flavor and allows the flavors to blend. Puttanesca sauce originates in Naples, Italy, but most versions don't include mussels. This underused seafood is full of protein and minerals that help support the immune system and metabolism. The best part is, when you use precooked frozen mussels, this comes together in 30 minutes or less.

1 tablespoon extra-virgin
olive oil

2 garlic cloves, minced

¼ teaspoon red pepper
flakes

1 (28-ounce) can
low-sodium crushed
tomatoes

1 tablespoon tomato paste

¼ cup chopped kalamata
olives

1 tablespoon capers

¼ teaspoon freshly ground
pepper

2 (8-ounce) packages
frozen, precooked
mussels

1 pound whole wheat
spaghetti

½ cup chopped fresh
parsley (optional)

1. In a large pot, heat the oil over medium heat. Add the garlic and red pepper flakes, and cook for 30 seconds, or until fragrant.

2. Stir in the crushed tomatoes and tomato paste and bring them to a boil.

3. Once boiling, reduce the heat to medium-low, and stir in the kalamata olives, capers, pepper, and mussels, cover, and simmer for 20 minutes, stirring occasionally.

4. While the sauce is cooking, cook the spaghetti according to package instructions. Drain the noodles, then add them to the sauce, tossing to coat.

5. Top with parsley (if using) and serve.

INGREDIENT TIP: Purchasing frozen, precooked mussels is a big time-saver and super affordable. Look for them in the frozen food aisle in the seafood section of your grocery store.

Per Serving: Calories: 534; Fat: 7g; Protein: 24g; Carbohydrates: 102g; Fiber: 13g; Sugar: 9g; Sodium: 594mg

CRAB-STUFFED PORTABELLA MUSHROOMS

Serves 6 / Prep time: 10 minutes / **Cook time:** 35 minutes

ONE-POT

I've turned one of my favorite appetizers into a crowd-pleasing main dish. Using canned seafood options helps keep this more affordable, but you can also take advantage of sales for seafood options you want to try.

6 portabella mushroom caps

1 small yellow onion, finely chopped

3 garlic cloves, minced

2 (10-ounce) cans crabmeat, drained

2 large eggs

⅓ cup Italian bread crumbs, divided

½ cup low-fat Greek yogurt

⅓ cup grated Parmesan cheese, divided

¼ cup chopped fresh basil

2 tablespoons freshly squeezed lemon juice

1 teaspoon salt

1. Preheat the oven to 425°F. Line a rimmed baking sheet with aluminum foil.

2. Wipe the mushroom caps with a damp paper towel, remove the stems, and scrape out the gills with a spoon.

3. Place the mushrooms gill-side down on the prepared baking sheet. Bake for 10 to 15 minutes, or until the mushrooms are tender.

4. While the mushrooms are baking, prepare the filling. In a large bowl, mix the onion, garlic, crabmeat, eggs, ½ cup bread crumbs, yogurt, ¼ cup Parmesan cheese, basil, lemon juice, and salt.

5. When the mushrooms are tender, remove them from the oven. Fill each mushroom cap with the crab mixture and sprinkle the remaining bread crumbs and Parmesan cheese over the top. Return the stuffed mushroom caps to the oven.

6. Bake for 15 to 20 minutes, or until the crab is heated through and the bread crumbs are golden brown.

VARIATION TIP: You can substitute any of your favorite seafood options, such as scallops, clams, or mussels, for the crab. Make them into easy appetizers by replacing the portabellas with button mushrooms.

Per Serving (1 stuffed mushroom): Calories: 189; Fat: 5g; Protein: 22g; Carbohydrates: 14g; Fiber: 2g; Sugar: 5g; Sodium: 951mg

CITRUS-POACHED COD

Serves 4 / **Prep time:** 10 minutes / **Cook time:** 15 minutes

DAIRY-FREE, QUICK

Poaching is a cooking method that sounds fancy and complicated, but it is as easy as simmering water. Cooking the cod in a bath of citrus-infused broth produces a delicate and moist fish that will seriously change how you prepare seafood from here on out.

FOR THE COD
1 orange, sliced

1 lemon, sliced

1½ cups low-sodium chicken broth

4 (4-ounce) skinless cod fillets

¼ cup chopped fresh parsley

FOR THE SAUCE
1 tablespoon extra-virgin olive oil

1 garlic clove, minced

Juice and grated zest of 1 orange

¼ teaspoon salt

1. **To make the cod:** In a large sauté pan, combine the orange slices, lemon slices, and broth, and bring to a boil over high heat.

2. Once boiling, add the cod. Reduce the heat to medium-low, cover, and simmer for 8 to 12 minutes, or until the cod is opaque and flakes easily with a fork.

3. **To make the sauce:** While the cod is cooking, in a small saucepan, heat the oil over medium-low heat. Add the garlic and cook for 30 seconds, or until fragrant.

4. Add the orange juice, orange zest, and salt, and reduce the heat to low. Simmer until the cod in the sauté pan is cooked.

5. Using a fish spatula, carefully transfer the fish to a serving dish, and top with the sliced oranges and lemons from the poaching liquid.

6. Pour the orange sauce over the cod and top with parsley before serving.

INGREDIENT TIP: Frozen cod can be used in place of fresh. Thaw each frozen fillet in the refrigerator overnight, and pat completely dry with a paper towel before cooking.

Per Serving (1 cod fillet with orange sauce): Calories: 135; Fat: 4g; Protein: 21g; Carbohydrates: 3g; Fiber: 0g; Sugar: 2g; Sodium: 209mg

SPAGHETTI WITH TOMATOES AND SARDINES

Serves 4 / Prep time: 10 minutes / **Cook time:** 20 minutes

DAIRY-FREE, QUICK

Sardines aren't as much of a staple in American cooking as in Mediterranean cooking, but they deserve as much love and respect as tuna. They are not only an affordable protein source but also full of heart-healthy fats and minerals like selenium and phosphorus that are important for immunity and bone health.

1 (16-ounce) box whole wheat spaghetti

1 tablespoon extra-virgin olive oil

½ red onion, chopped

2 garlic cloves, minced

1 (28-ounce) can low-sodium diced tomatoes

2 (4-ounce) tins skinless, boneless sardines in tomato sauce

½ cup sliced black olives

1 tablespoon capers

¼ teaspoon red pepper flakes

½ cup chopped fresh basil

1. Cook the spaghetti according to the package instructions. Drain the noodles, return them to the pot, and set them aside.

2. While the pasta is cooking, make the sauce. In a medium saucepan, heat the oil over medium heat.

3. Add the onion and cook for 3 to 4 minutes, or until softened. Add the garlic and cook for an additional 30 seconds. Stir in the tomatoes, sardines, olives, capers, and red pepper flakes, and reduce the heat to low. Cover and simmer for 10 minutes.

4. Pour the sauce into the pot with the spaghetti and stir to combine. Divide between four plates. Top with the basil and serve.

SUBSTITUTION TIP: Still not a fan of sardines? You can also make this with other kinds of canned seafood, such as tuna, salmon, mackerel, or clams.

Per Serving: Calories: 578; Fat: 13g; Protein: 29g; Carbohydrates: 95g; Fiber: 14g; Sugar: 6g; Sodium: 449mg

Herbed Lamb Chops with Lemon-Rosemary Dressing, **page 102**

POULTRY AND MEAT

HERB-MARINATED CHICKEN SKEWERS

Serves 4 / **Prep time:** 10 minutes, plus 30 minutes to marinate / **Cook time:** 15 minutes

DAIRY-FREE, ONE-POT

Inspired by Greek souvlakis and cookbook authors Kenton and Jane Kotsiris, these chicken skewers get their delicious flavor from a simple herb marinade. You can cook these skewers on an outdoor grill during the warmer months or on the stovetop in a cast-iron skillet when it's too cold to grill. Serve these skewers with a side of vegetable pilaf, couscous, or sandwich-style, stuffed into a pita with shredded lettuce, diced tomatoes, and a spoonful of Greek yogurt.

¼ cup extra-virgin olive oil

Grated zest of 1 lemon

Juice of 2 lemons, about ½ cup

1 tablespoon dried oregano

½ tablespoon dried thyme

3 garlic cloves, minced

½ teaspoon salt

¼ teaspoon freshly ground black pepper

3 pounds boneless, skinless chicken breasts, cut into 2-inch cubes

Stainless steel skewers

1. In a large bowl with a resealable lid, mix the oil, lemon zest, lemon juice, oregano, thyme, garlic, salt, and pepper. Add the chicken to the herb marinade and stir to coat. Cover the bowl and refrigerate for 20 to 30 minutes.

2. Remove the chicken from the refrigerator, and thread the chicken pieces onto the skewers, about 4 to 5 pieces per skewer. Discard the marinade.

3. Heat a large cast-iron skillet over medium-high heat. Place 3 to 4 skewers in the skillet, and cook for 5 to 7 minutes, turning until the chicken is cooked through and a food thermometer inserted into the thickest part of the chicken reaches an internal temperature of 165°F. Repeat with the remaining skewers until all are cooked, and serve.

VARIATION TIP: For added vegetables and color, alternate the chicken with chunks of bell pepper, zucchini, or onion on each skewer before cooking.

Per Serving: Calories: 519; Fat: 19g; Protein: 79g; Carbohydrates: 3g; Fiber: 1g; Sugar: 1g; Sodium: 532mg

LAMB AND MUSHROOM MEATBALLS WITH YOGURT SAUCE

Serves 4 / Prep time: 10 minutes / **Cook time:** 25 minutes

My husband's favorite dumplings from a local Turkish restaurant inspired these meatballs. My secret twist? Adding mushrooms! Finely chopped mushrooms resemble ground meat, and adding them to the meatballs is an easy way to boost nutrition and moisture. Serve these meatballs with cooked rice, roasted potatoes, or a pita sandwich smothered with plenty of yogurt sauce.

FOR THE MEATBALLS

½ pound button
  mushrooms

½ small yellow onion

1 garlic clove

1 pound ground lamb

½ cup whole wheat
  bread crumbs

1 large egg

½ teaspoon ground cumin

½ teaspoon paprika

½ teaspoon ground
  cinnamon

FOR THE YOGURT SAUCE

1 cup low-fat plain
  Greek yogurt

½ cup chopped fresh mint

1 tablespoon freshly
  squeezed lemon juice

1. **To make the meatballs:** In a food processor, pulse the mushrooms until finely chopped.

2. Heat a large oven-safe or cast-iron skillet over medium-high heat. Put the mushrooms into the hot skillet and cook until all water is released, 2 to 3 minutes. Remove the mushrooms from the heat and let cool.

3. Preheat the oven to 400°F.

4. Put the onion and garlic into the food processor and pulse until they are finely chopped. Transfer the onion and garlic mixture to a large bowl. Add the ground lamb, bread crumbs, egg, cumin, paprika, cinnamon, and cooled mushrooms to the onion and garlic.

5. Heat the same cast-iron skillet on medium heat. Using clean hands, form the lamb mixture into 12 meatballs. Put the meatballs into the hot skillet and brown each side for 1 to 2 minutes.

6. Cover the skillet with aluminum foil and transfer it to the oven. Bake for 20 minutes, or until cooked through, and a food thermometer inserted into the largest meatball registers 165°F. Let cool for 5 minutes before serving.

7. **To make the yogurt sauce:** In a small bowl, mix the yogurt, mint, and lemon juice. Serve the sauce alongside the cooked meatballs.

SUBSTITUTION TIP: Instead of lamb, make these meatballs with ground beef or ground turkey for a leaner and less-expensive option.

Per Serving (3 meatballs with yogurt sauce): Calories: 328; Fat: 17g; Protein: 31g; Carbohydrates: 14g; Fiber: 2g; Sugar: 6g; Sodium: 183mg

HERBED LAMB CHOPS WITH LEMON-ROSEMARY DRESSING

Serves 6 / **Prep time:** 5 minutes, plus 1 hour to marinate and 15 minutes to rest / **Cook time:** 10 minutes

DAIRY-FREE, ONE-POT

Lamb chops can seem intimidating, but they can be simple to flavor and cook if you know the right way to prepare them. This lamb dish inspired by cookbook author Denise Hazime combines the bright flavor from the lemon and fresh herbs with the smoky flavor from grilling. This cut of meat can be on the pricier side, so take advantage of store sales, or save this dish for those special-occasion meals, because it is worth the splurge.

1 cup freshly squeezed
　　lemon juice

¾ cup extra-virgin olive oil

¼ cup fresh rosemary

3 garlic cloves

1 teaspoon salt

½ teaspoon freshly ground
　　black pepper

6 lamb chops, 1 inch thick

1. In a food processor, blend the lemon juice, oil, rosemary, garlic, salt, and pepper for 15 seconds. Set aside.

2. Put the lamb chops in a large plastic zip-top bag or container with a resealable lid. Cover the lamb with two-thirds of the dressing, ensuring that all the lamb chops are fully coated. Let the lamb marinate in the refrigerator for at least 1 hour.

3. Remove the lamb chops from the refrigerator and let them sit at room temperature for 15 minutes. Heat a grill, grill pan, or cast-iron skillet to high heat.

4. Cook the lamb chops for 2 minutes on each side for medium-rare or 3 minutes per side for medium. Let rest 5 minutes before serving.

5. Serve by drizzling the reserved dressing over the lamb.

SHOPPING TIP: Look for lamb shoulder chops for a less-expensive option. These require at least 3 to 4 minutes of cooking per side.

Per Serving: Calories: 505; Fat: 46g; Protein: 22g; Carbohydrates: 1g; Fiber: 0g; Sugar: 0g; Sodium: 219mg

ZA'ATAR ROASTED CHICKEN THIGHS

Serves 6 / Prep time: 5 minutes / **Cook time:** 20 minutes

5 INGREDIENTS OR FEWER, DAIRY-FREE, ONE-POT, QUICK

Za'atar (*zah-tar*) is a spice blend popular in Middle Eastern cuisine that includes spices such as oregano, sumac, marjoram, and sesame seeds. Using a spice blend such as za'atar is an easy way to add a punch of flavor with minimal time and effort. Chicken thighs are often less expensive than chicken breasts, especially when buying a bulk-style family pack. Serve this chicken with roasted root vegetables or Garlic Parmesan Smashed Brussels Sprouts (page 53).

6 boneless, skinless chicken thighs

1 tablespoon extra-virgin olive oil

1 tablespoon za'atar seasoning

1 teaspoon garlic powder

1. Preheat the oven to 375°F. Line a baking sheet with aluminum foil or parchment paper.

2. Arrange the chicken thighs on the baking sheet and coat each with oil.

3. In a small bowl, mix the za'atar seasoning and garlic powder.

4. Sprinkle the seasoning mixture onto the chicken thighs and press it down into the meat with clean hands, so it adheres.

5. Bake for 15 to 20 minutes, or until a food thermometer inserted into the thickest part of each chicken thigh registers 165°F. Let rest for 2 to 3 minutes before serving.

INGREDIENT TIP: If you can't find za'atar, use 1 teaspoon of oregano, thyme, and sesame seeds instead.

Per Serving (1 seasoned chicken thigh): Calories: 193; Fat: 8g; Protein: 28g; Carbohydrates: 0g; Fiber: 0g; Sugar: 0g; Sodium: 135mg

SUN-DRIED TOMATO AND ARUGULA STUFFED CHICKEN BREASTS

Serves 4 / Prep time: 10 minutes / **Cook time:** 20 minutes

ONE-POT, QUICK

Stuffed chicken is an easy yet impressive main dish that will please any honored guest and your midweek dinner crowd just the same. Using sun-dried tomatoes packed in oil adds extra moisture and Mediterranean-inspired flavor. Serve this with vegetables such as sautéed green beans, asparagus, or a simple green salad.

4 boneless, skinless chicken breasts

1½ cups arugula, finely chopped

½ cup sun-dried tomatoes packed in oil, chopped

¼ cup plus 2 tablespoons grated Parmesan cheese

2 garlic cloves, minced

½ cup Italian bread crumbs

1 tablespoon extra-virgin olive oil

1. Preheat the oven to 350°F. Line a baking sheet with aluminum foil or parchment paper and set it aside.

2. Cut a deep pocket into the side of each chicken breast.

3. In a medium bowl, mix the arugula, sun-dried tomatoes, ¼ cup of Parmesan cheese, and the garlic.

4. Stuff each chicken breast with the arugula mixture. Use toothpicks to seal each pocket, then transfer the stuffed chicken breasts to the prepared baking sheet.

5. In a small bowl, mix the bread crumbs and the remaining 2 tablespoons of Parmesan cheese.

6. Coat each chicken breast with oil and coat each with the bread crumb mixture, pressing to make the bread crumbs adhere.

7. Bake for 20 minutes, or until a food thermometer inserted into the thickest part of each chicken breast registers 165°F.

8. Let the chicken rest for 2 minutes. Remove the toothpicks before serving.

SUBSTITUTION TIP: Make this dairy-free by omitting the cheese from the breading and replacing the cheese in the filling with finely chopped walnuts or garlic hummus.

Per Serving (1 stuffed chicken breast): Calories: 251; Fat: 10g; Protein: 30g; Carbohydrates: 10g; Fiber: 1g; Sugar: 1g; Sodium: 301mg

BULGUR AND TURKEY STUFFED ZUCCHINI

Serves 6 / **Prep time:** 10 minutes / **Cook time:** 30 minutes

DAIRY-FREE

Bulgur, a grain made from cracked wheat, is a popular ingredient in many Mediterranean and Middle Eastern dishes, but it may be most popular in the Lebanese dish tabbouleh. Its nutty flavor gives these stuffed zucchinis delicious flavor, as well as fiber and minerals.

6 medium zucchini

1 pound lean ground turkey

1 yellow onion, chopped

1 red bell pepper, seeded and finely chopped

1 cup low-sodium chicken broth

½ cup bulgur

1 teaspoon dried oregano

½ teaspoon salt

½ teaspoon dried dill

1. Preheat the oven to 400°F.

2. Halve each zucchini lengthwise. Scoop out and reserve the flesh in a small bowl, leaving a ¼-inch-thick border around the edge to maintain the shape of the zucchini.

3. Arrange the zucchini halves cut-side down in an 11-by-13-inch baking dish. Bake the zucchini halves for 10 to 15 minutes or until tender. Remove the zucchini from the oven and set it aside.

4. While the zucchini is baking, heat a large skillet or sauté pan over medium heat. Add the ground turkey, and cook for 5 minutes, or until fully browned.

5. Stir in the onion, bell pepper, and reserved zucchini flesh, and cook for another 3 minutes, or until softened.

6. Add the chicken broth to the pan and bring it to a boil. Stir in the bulgur, oregano, salt, and dill. Reduce the heat to low and simmer for 12 to 15 minutes, or until the bulgur is tender.

7. Spoon the turkey mixture into the baked zucchini halves, cover with aluminum foil, and bake for an additional 10 minutes. Remove from the oven and serve.

SHOPPING TIP: Chicken broth often goes on sale, especially during the holidays. Stock up on this pantry staple during sales for extra cost savings.

Per Serving: Calories: 201; Fat: 7g; Protein: 18g; Carbohydrates: 18g; Fiber: 4g; Sugar: 7g; Sodium: 265mg

HARISSA-SPICED TURKEY BURGERS WITH TZATZIKI

Serves 4 / Prep time: 10 minutes **/ Cook time:** 10 minutes

ONE-POT, QUICK

Harissa, which translates from the Arabic verb meaning "to pound or break into pieces," is a paste made from chilies, salt, oil, and spices. It is a condiment in North Africa and an ingredient in dishes such as stews, meat dishes, and couscous. It is also available in a spice blend, which gives these burgers some serious kick. Don't worry, though, the tzatziki topping helps balance out the heat.

1 pound lean ground turkey

½ yellow onion, chopped

2 garlic cloves, minced

1 teaspoon ground cumin

1 tablespoon harissa seasoning

1 teaspoon salt

2 teaspoons extra-virgin olive oil

4 whole wheat hamburger buns, for serving

1 batch Easy Tzatziki (page 140), or store-bought tzatziki

Arugula

1. In a large mixing bowl, combine the ground turkey, onion, garlic, cumin, harissa seasoning, and salt. Using clean hands, form the turkey mixture into four patties.

2. In a large skillet, heat the oil over medium heat. Place the turkey patties into the hot skillet, and cook them for 4 to 5 minutes per side, or until browned and a thermometer inserted into the thickest part of each patty registers 165°F.

3. Serve in hamburger buns and top the patties with Easy Tzatziki and arugula.

VARIATION TIP: Want extra spice? Add ¼ teaspoon of red pepper flakes to the ground turkey before cooking.

Per Serving (1 turkey burger with tzatziki and arugula):
Calories: 390; Fat: 18g; Protein: 29g; Carbohydrates: 30g; Fiber: 4g; Sugar: 7g; Sodium: 934mg

TZATZIKI PORK CHOPS

Serves 6 / Prep time: 10 minutes, plus 30 minutes to marinate / **Cook time:** 25 minutes

ONE-POT

Tzatziki isn't just a delicious dip for vegetables or sauce for pita sandwiches. It is an excellent marinade for meat. Baking pork chops smothered in tzatziki locks in the flavor and moisture of the meat. This hearty dish pairs well with sautéed greens, baked potatoes, sliced into a pita, or over a green salad. Save some tzatziki for dipping!

6 (5-ounce) boneless pork
   chops
1 cup Easy Tzatziki
   (page 140), or store-
   bought tzatziki

1. Place the pork chops in a resealable container and smother them with the tzatziki. Toss to coat the meat evenly. Refrigerate for 30 minutes to 1 hour.

2. Preheat the oven to 400°F. Line a baking sheet with aluminum foil or parchment paper.

3. Arrange the marinated pork chops on the prepared baking sheet, then bake them for 15 to 20 minutes, or until a food thermometer inserted into the thickest part of the pork registers 145°F. Let rest for 5 minutes before serving.

INGREDIENT TIP: Make sure that the pork chops are the same thickness for even cooking time. If needed, place the pork chops in a resealable plastic bag and pound them with a tenderizer to desired thickness.

Per Serving (1 marinated pork chop): Calories: 298; Fat: 14g; Protein: 35g; Carbohydrates: 6g; Sugar: 6g; Sodium: 412mg

SPICY PORK AND ZUCCHINI PASTA

Serves 6 / Prep time: 10 minutes / **Cook time:** 20 minutes

DAIRY-FREE, QUICK

It's time to add a little fire to dinner with this pasta dish. The red pepper flakes and cayenne pepper add some serious kick, which can be adjusted up or down to suit any heat level you like. Using ground pork instead of the usual beef or turkey imparts great flavor and is also a source of energy-boosting B vitamins and iron.

1 pound whole wheat rotini

1 tablespoon extra-virgin olive oil

1 yellow onion, chopped

2 garlic cloves, minced

1 pound lean ground pork

2 medium zucchini, sliced

1 teaspoon salt

1 teaspoon dried oregano

½ or ⅓ teaspoon red pepper flakes

¼ teaspoon cayenne pepper

1 (15-ounce) can stewed tomatoes

1 (15-ounce) fire-roasted tomatoes

1. Cook the pasta according to the package instructions. Drain the noodles, return them to the pot, and set them aside.

2. While the pasta is cooking, in a large sauté pan, heat the oil over medium-high heat. Add the onion and garlic and cook for 3 to 4 minutes, or until the onion has softened.

3. Add the ground pork to the pan and continue cooking until the pork is browned and cooked through.

4. Stir in the zucchini, salt, oregano, red pepper flakes, and cayenne pepper, and continue cooking for 5 minutes, or until the zucchini has softened.

5. Add the stewed tomatoes and fire-roasted tomatoes. Reduce the heat to medium-low and simmer the sauce for 5 minutes.

6. Pour the sauce over the cooked pasta. Stir to coat the noodles in the sauce and serve.

VARIATION TIP: Turn up the heat by adding a chopped jalapeño pepper or a few dashes of your favorite hot sauce when adding the zucchini to the sauce in step 3.

Per Serving: Calories: 428; Fat: 7g; Protein: 30g; Carbohydrates: 168g; Fiber: 11g; Sugar: 8g; Sodium: 478mg

MARINATED PORK LOIN WITH OLIVE TAPENADE

Serves 4 / **Prep time:** 10 minutes, plus 1 hour to marinate / **Cook time:** 20 minutes

DAIRY-FREE, ONE-POT

Packed with Mediterranean-inspired flavors, these pork loins are marinated in Greek dressing then topped with a briny olive tapenade. You can prep the dressing and tapenade ahead of time and marinate the pork the night before, so when it's time for dinner, all that's left to do is bake and eat. Serve with a side of roasted potatoes, grilled asparagus, or Warm Lentil Salad (page 55).

FOR THE PORK

4 (4-ounce) boneless pork loins

1 cup Greek salad dressing

FOR THE TAPENADE

1 cup sliced black olives

1 cup pitted kalamata olives

¼ cup extra-virgin olive oil

2 garlic cloves

1 tablespoon capers

1 tablespoon freshly squeezed lemon juice

½ cup chopped fresh basil, divided

1. **To make the pork:** Put the pork loins and Greek dressing in a resealable zip-top bag or a bowl with a lid. Toss to coat the pork with dressing, and refrigerate for at least 1 hour, or up to overnight.

2. **To make the tapenade:** In a food processor, combine the black olives, kalamata olives, oil, garlic, capers, lemon juice, and ¼ cup basil. Pulse until finely chopped or it is the desired texture. Refrigerate the tapenade in a resealable container until ready to use.

3. Preheat the oven to 375°F. Line a baking sheet with aluminum foil.

4. Arrange the marinated pork loins on the prepared baking sheet, brushing each with more marinade. Discard the rest of the marinade. Bake the pork for 20 minutes, or until cooked through, and a food thermometer inserted into the thickest part of the pork registers 145°F. Let the pork rest for 5 minutes.

5. Top each pork chop with olive tapenade and the remaining ¼ cup of basil and serve.

INGREDIENT TIP: If pork loins are too thick, or aren't the same thickness, put them in a zip-top bag, and pound with a meat tenderizer or rolling pin to reach your desired thickness.

Per Serving (1 pork chop with olive tapenade): Calories: 460; Fat: 36g; Protein: 25g; Carbohydrates: 9g; Fiber: 2g; Sugar: 3g; Sodium: 780mg

GREEK-INSPIRED BEEF PITAS

Serves 4 / Prep time: 12 minutes / **Cook time:** 15 minutes

ONE-POT, QUICK

These pita sandwiches are quick and easy to prepare. When you first bite into these sandwiches, you might think of gyros—a popular Greek street food commonly made with roasted beef or lamb. You can serve these up taco-style, put all the ingredients on top of the pita, and fold it in half to eat, or cut the pita in half and stuff each as a pocket-style sandwich. Bonus points if you prepare a batch of tzatziki ahead of time.

1 tablespoon extra-virgin olive oil

1 small yellow onion, chopped

2 garlic cloves, minced

1 pound lean ground beef

1 teaspoon dried oregano

½ teaspoon salt

4 (8-inch) whole wheat pita rounds

1 batch Easy Tzatziki (page 140), or store-bought tzatziki

½ English cucumber, sliced

1 large tomato, chopped

¼ cup crumbled feta cheese

1. In a large skillet, heat the oil over medium heat. Add the onion, and cook for 3 minutes, or until the onion has softened. Add the garlic and cook for an additional 30 seconds, or until fragrant.

2. Add the ground beef to the skillet and cook for 5 to 7 minutes, or until it is cooked through and browned. Stir in the oregano and salt, then remove the pan from the heat.

3. Put the cooked beef into each pita round. Top with the tzatziki, cucumber, tomato, and feta before serving.

SUBSTITUTION TIP: If you don't have any tzatziki on hand, you can top your pita with a dollop of low-fat Greek yogurt or sour cream in a pinch.

Per Serving (1 pita sandwich): Calories: 522; Fat: 22g; Protein: 35g; Carbohydrates: 47g; Fiber: 6g; Sugar: 10g; Sodium: 934mg

BEEF AND TOMATO STEW

Serves 6 / **Prep time:** 10 minutes / **Cook time:** 1 hour 30 minutes

DAIRY-FREE, ONE-POT, WORTH THE WAIT

Featuring the flavors of Spain, this stew has a tempting flavor that comes from simmering slow and low on the stove. Chuck roast is an affordable beef cut, but it requires a longer cooking time to tenderize. Slow cooking makes the beef more tender and allows the flavors of all the ingredients to develop fully. Serve this on a bed of rice or with a side of whole-grain bread for dipping.

2 pounds beef chuck roast, cubed

1 red bell pepper, seeded and chopped

2 carrots, sliced

4 garlic cloves, minced

2 teaspoons smoked paprika

1 teaspoon dried oregano

½ teaspoon salt

1 (28-ounce) can low-sodium crushed tomatoes

1 (28-ounce) can fire-roasted diced tomatoes

1 (14-ounce) can low-sodium beef broth

2 tablespoons tomato paste

½ cup pitted green olives

1 cup frozen peas (optional)

1. Heat a large pot over medium heat.

2. Put the beef chuck roast into the pot and cook for 5 minutes, or until browned.

3. Add the bell pepper, carrots, and garlic, and cook for 3 minutes or until the vegetables soften. Stir in the paprika, oregano, and salt, and cook for an additional 30 seconds.

4. Add the crushed tomatoes, diced tomatoes, beef broth, and tomato paste, and bring to a boil.

5. Reduce the heat to low, and simmer for 1 hour, 20 minutes, stirring intermittently.

6. Stir in the olives and peas (if using) and cook for an additional minute. Remove from the heat and serve.

INGREDIENT TIP: To make it easier to chop the beef, freeze it for up to 1 hour before cutting.

Per Serving: Calories: 384; Fat: 21g; Protein: 33g; Carbohydrates: 20g; Fiber: 7g; Sugar: 12g; Sodium: 810mg

STEAK AND SWISS CHARD SANDWICHES WITH ROASTED GARLIC SAUCE

Serves 6 / Prep time: 10 minutes, plus 10 minutes to chill / **Cook time:** 10 minutes

ONE-POT, QUICK

If you're a fan of garlic, you've come to the right place. These sandwiches pack a serious garlicky punch with every bite, which you can add to just about anything with the quick and easy garlic sauce. The Swiss chard, a leafy green, is rich in vitamins A and K, important nutrients for eye health and metabolism.

½ cup low-fat milk

3 tablespoons freshly squeezed lemon juice

2 cloves Roasted Garlic (page 135)

1 teaspoon Dijon mustard

½ teaspoon salt, divided

½ cup extra-virgin olive oil

1½ pounds sirloin tip roast, thinly sliced

¼ teaspoon freshly ground black pepper

3 cups chopped Swiss chard, stems removed

6 whole wheat hamburger buns

1. In a high-powered blender or food processor, combine the milk, lemon juice, garlic, mustard, and ¼ teaspoon of salt. Blend on low until mixed.

2. While the sauce is still blending, stream in the oil very slowly until the sauce starts to thicken. Pour it into a jar with a lid, cover, and refrigerate for at least 10 minutes.

3. While the sauce is chilling, heat a large skillet over medium heat. Add the sliced sirloin, the remaining ¼ teaspoon of salt, the black pepper, and the Swiss chard. Cook for 5 to 7 minutes, or until the beef is cooked through and the chard is wilted.

4. Divide the mixture evenly between the six hamburger bun bottoms. Drizzle garlic sauce over each one, then top with tops of the hamburger buns before serving.

SUBSTITUTION TIP: To make dairy-free, replace the milk in the garlic sauce with your favorite nondairy milk alternative.

Per Serving (1 sandwich): Calories: 467; Fat: 29g; Protein: 28g; Carbohydrates: 25g; Fiber: 4g; Sugar: 5g; Sodium: 535mg

SPICED GROUND BEEF AND EGGPLANT COUSCOUS BOWLS

Serves 4 / Prep time: 10 minutes / **Cook time:** 20 minutes

DAIRY-FREE, QUICK

These bowls would fit in nicely in Morocco, where couscous is a staple dish, and spices like cumin and paprika are prominent flavors. Adding red wine vinegar to the beef gives a bit of a tang that balances out the earthy spices for maximum flavor.

2 cups low-sodium chicken
   broth, divided

1½ cups uncooked
   couscous

1 tablespoon extra-virgin
   olive oil

1 yellow onion, chopped

1 red bell pepper, seeded
   and chopped

3 garlic cloves, minced

1 pound lean ground beef

1 medium eggplant, peeled
   and chopped

2 teaspoons ground cumin

1 teaspoon smoked
   paprika

2 tablespoons tomato
   paste

2 tablespoons red wine
   vinegar

Salt (optional)

½ cup chopped fresh
   parsley (optional)

1. In a large saucepan set over high heat, bring 1¾ cups of the chicken broth to a boil. Stir in the couscous, cover, and remove from the heat. Let the couscous sit for 5 minutes, then fluff it with a fork.

2. Meanwhile, in a large skillet, heat the oil over medium heat. Add the onion and bell pepper, and cook, stirring occasionally, for 4 to 5 minutes, or until the vegetables have softened.

3. Stir in the garlic and cook for an additional 30 seconds before adding the ground beef. Cook the beef until browned and cooked through, about 4 minutes.

4. Stir in the eggplant, cumin, and paprika and cook for 3 minutes more, or until the eggplant starts to soften.

5. Reduce the heat to medium-low, and stir in the tomato paste, vinegar, and the remaining ¼ cup of chicken broth. Simmer for 5 minutes, then remove the skillet from the heat. Taste and adjust the seasonings as needed.

6. Divide the couscous evenly between four bowls. Top with the beef mixture and the parsley (if using) before serving.

SUBSTITUTION TIP: This dish can be made with ground lamb or turkey in place of the beef. You can also substitute cilantro for parsley for a different flavor.

Per Serving: Calories: 525; Fat: 16g; Protein: 34g; Carbohydrates: 66g; Fiber: 9g; Sugar: 8g; Sodium: 194mg

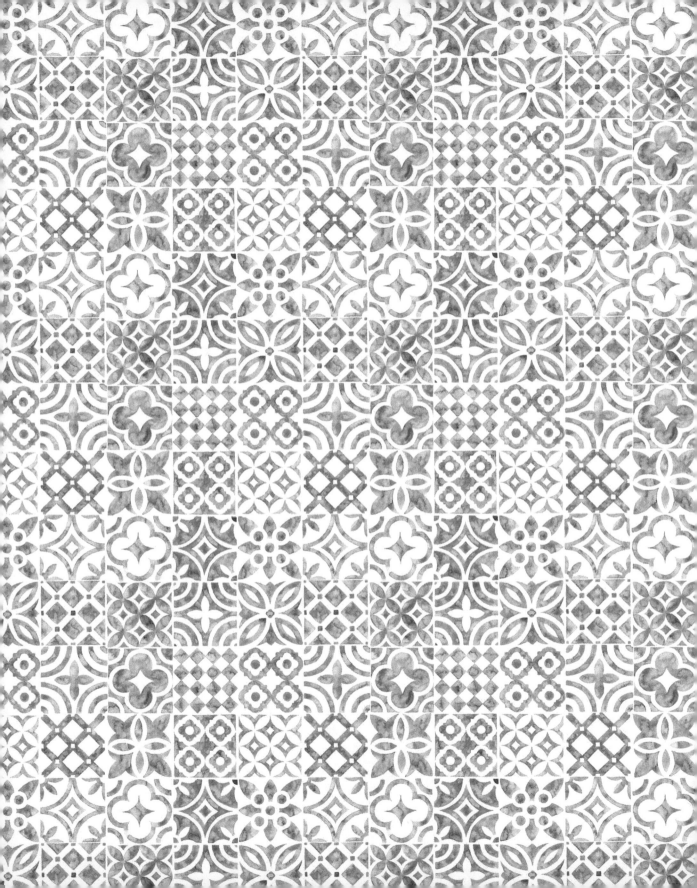

Watermelon and Mint Salad, page 122

DESSERTS

RED WINE AND ORANGE—POACHED PEARS

Serves 4 / **Prep time:** 5 minutes / **Cook time:** 35 minutes

5 INGREDIENTS OR FEWER, DAIRY-FREE, VEGETARIAN

My French heritage and a recipe from chef Sanaa Abourezk motivated me to create these elegant pears, ideal for a showstopping dessert at your next dinner party. Your guests don't need to know how easy they were to prepare. The red wine gives them a gorgeous crimson hue. Serve these pears alongside some softened Brie cheese or with a dollop of fresh whipped cream.

**4 cups dry red wine or
   cranberry juice**

½ cup sugar

½ cup dried cranberries

**Juice and grated zest of
   1 orange**

**4 firm, ripe pears, peeled
   with the stems intact**

1. In a large saucepan over medium heat, combine the red wine, sugar, cranberries, orange juice, and orange zest, and bring them to a boil.

2. Reduce the heat to low, and simmer for 5 minutes. Meanwhile, slice ¼ to ½ inch off the bottom of each pear, so it stands upright. Using tongs, gently lower each pear into the simmering liquid.

3. Cover and simmer for 15 minutes, turning the pears every 5 minutes to color them evenly, until the pears are cooked but still firm.

4. Remove the pears from the cooking liquid and place them on a platter. Set them aside.

5. Continue to cook the liquid for 5 to 10 minutes more, or until thickened and slightly syrupy.

6. Remove the liquid from the heat, let it cool for about 5 minutes, then drizzle it over the pears and serve.

VARIATION TIP: Use white wine, lemon, and vanilla in place of the red wine, cranberries, and orange for a different flavor experience.

Per Serving (1 poached pear): Calories: 335; Fat: 1g; Protein: 1g; Carbohydrates: 71g; Fiber: 7g; Sugar: 40g; Sodium: 8mg

CREAMY BANANA DATE SHAKE

Serves 1 to 2 / Prep time: 5 minutes

5 INGREDIENTS OR FEWER, QUICK, VEGETARIAN

You're going to want to break out the big straw for this shake. Using a frozen banana and dates gives it a naturally sweet flavor and a thick and creamy texture. You can adjust the amount of milk depending on how thick you want the shake to be.

1 frozen banana

½ or ⅓ cup low-fat milk or nondairy milk

2 or 3 pitted dates

1 teaspoon vanilla extract

¼ teaspoon ground cinnamon

1. In a blender, combine the banana, milk, dates, vanilla, and cinnamon. Use ½ cup of milk if you like a thicker shake and ¾ cup if you like it thinner.

2. Blend on high for 1 minute or until creamy.

3. Pour the mixture into serving glasses and serve.

SHOPPING TIP: Look for pitted dates in the baking aisle, which tend to be more affordable options than those found in the produce section.

Per Serving (1 cup): Calories: 210; Fat: 2g; Protein: 6g; Carbohydrates: 45g; Fiber: 5g; Sugar: 30g; Sodium: 56mg

WATERMELON AND MINT SALAD

Serves 6 to 8 / Prep time: 10 minutes

5 INGREDIENTS OR FEWER, DAIRY-FREE, QUICK, VEGETARIAN

This refreshing dessert can double as a snack, especially when watermelon is in season and on sale during summer days. The pop of mint adds an extra dose of cool refreshment for humid days, especially after it's been chilling in the refrigerator for a bit.

8 cups seedless
watermelon, diced into
1-inch cubes

1 cup fresh blueberries

¼ cup chopped fresh mint
leaves

¼ cup freshly squeezed
lime juice

1 tablespoon honey
(optional)

1. Put the watermelon cubes in a large bowl and sprinkle the blueberries over the top.

2. In a small bowl, mix the mint, lime juice, and honey (if using).

3. Drizzle the mint dressing over the fruit and toss to coat.

4. Refrigerate until ready to serve.

VARIATION TIP: To serve this salad as a savory side or snack, add ½ cup cubed feta cheese in step 1 and a pinch of cayenne pepper in the dressing.

Per Serving: Calories: 238; Protein: 4g; Carbohydrates: 61g; Sugar: 52g; Fiber: 3g; Total fat: 1g; Sodium: 11mg

MICROWAVE APPLE CRISP FOR ONE

Serves 1 / Prep time: 10 minutes / **Cook time:** 2 minutes

DAIRY-FREE, QUICK, VEGETARIAN

Once autumn rolls around, apples are abundant, and the cool temperature hits, I immediately crave a bowl of warm apple crisp—no need to turn on the oven, or share, for that matter, with this recipe. Choose whichever apple varieties are on sale for extra savings, but a firm apple like Fuji, Gala, or Granny Smith works best.

1 large apple, peeled, cored, and sliced

1 teaspoon freshly squeezed lemon juice

¼ teaspoon vanilla extract

1 teaspoon whole wheat flour

1½ teaspoons packed light brown sugar

¼ teaspoon ground cinnamon

2 tablespoons low-sugar granola, divided

1. In a microwave-safe mug, combine the apple slices, lemon juice, vanilla, flour, brown sugar, and cinnamon. Stir until the apple slices are fully coated.

2. Top with 1½ tablespoons of the granola, and microwave on high for 1 to 2 minutes, or until the apples are soft.

3. Let cool in the microwave for 1 minute. Use an oven mitt to remove the mug carefully (the mug will be very hot).

4. Top with the remaining ½ tablespoon of granola and serve.

VARIATION TIP: Top with a dollop of fresh whipped cream or nondairy whipped topping for a little something extra.

Per Serving (1 apple crisp): Calories: 185; Fat: 1g; Protein: 2g; Carbohydrates: 46g; Fiber: 4g; Sugar: 29g; Sodium: 5mg

5-INGREDIENT OATMEAL RAISIN COOKIES

Makes 12 cookies / Prep time: 10 minutes / **Cook time:** 10 minutes

5 INGREDIENTS OR FEWER, DAIRY-FREE, QUICK, SUGAR-FREE, VEGETARIAN

If you ask me, you can't talk about desserts without cookies. Although these aren't like traditional cookies you had at Grandma's house, with extra butter and sugar, they have all the things I love in a good cookie and will satisfy any sweet tooth. Overripe bananas are used for sweetening, making these cookies both added-sugar-free and a money saver. What a combo!

1½ **cups rolled oats**

1½ **teaspoons ground cinnamon**

½ **teaspoon salt**

2 **overripe bananas, peeled**

1½ **teaspoons vanilla extract**

½ **cup raisins**

1. Preheat the oven to 350°F. Line a baking sheet with parchment paper. Set it aside.

2. In a large bowl, mix the oats, cinnamon, and salt.

3. In a medium bowl, mash the bananas with the vanilla. Stir the banana mixture into the oat mixture until the oats are moistened. Stir in the raisins.

4. For each cookie, drop a spoonful of the batter onto the prepared baking sheet. Using clean, greased hands, form each spoonful into 3-inch cookie rounds on the baking sheet.

5. Bake for 8 to 12 minutes or until the cookies are firm. Let cool on the baking sheet for 5 minutes before transferring to a wire cooling rack to cool completely.

6. Store in an airtight container for up to 4 days, or refrigerate for up to 1 week.

VARIATION TIP: Use any of your favorite dried fruits, such as dried cranberries, cherries, or apricots, in place of the raisins, or add ¼ cup of chopped nuts for some crunch.

Per Serving (1 cookie): Calories: 96; Fat: 1g; Protein: 3g; Carbohydrates: 20g; Fiber: 3g; Sugar: 7g; Sodium: 98mg

RICOTTA WITH ROASTED STRAWBERRIES

Serves 2 / Prep time: 5 minutes / **Cook time:** 25 minutes

5 INGREDIENTS OR FEWER, QUICK, VEGETARIAN

You may think you've had strawberries every way possible, but have you roasted them in the oven? Roasting boosts their sweetness and flavor, making them a perfect partner for creamy ricotta cheese. Best of all, you can get away with using frozen strawberries if fresh ones aren't in season or out of your budget. Simply bake them straight from frozen and increase the baking time by 5 to 10 minutes.

1 pound strawberries, washed and hulled

½ tablespoon sugar

1 teaspoon vanilla extract

1 cup part-skim ricotta cheese

1 teaspoon grated lemon zest

1. Preheat the oven to 350°F. Line a baking sheet with parchment paper. Set aside.

2. In a large bowl, mix the strawberries, sugar, and vanilla. Spread the strawberries onto the prepared baking sheet in an even layer, and roast for 25 minutes, or until they are soft and slightly browned. Let them cool for 5 minutes.

3. In a medium bowl, stir together the ricotta and lemon zest, then divide the mixture evenly between two serving bowls.

4. Top the ricotta with the roasted strawberries before serving.

VARIATION TIP: For extra depth of flavor, drizzle a little Balsamic Glaze (page 138) over the top or sprinkle with freshly chopped mint.

Per Serving: Calories: 262; Fat: 10g; Protein: 16g; Carbohydrates: 27g; Fiber: 5g; Sugar: 15g; Sodium: 125mg

PEAR AND CRANBERRY SALAD

Serves 4 / Prep time: 10 minutes

5 INGREDIENTS OR FEWER, QUICK, VEGETARIAN

I know the words *salad* and *dessert* don't usually go together, but this should be an exception. I make this pear and cranberry salad on repeat once the fall season begins, but it can be made any time of the year for dessert or even as a refreshing side dish for cookouts. You can easily replace the pears with apples if they are on sale or in season.

3 large Barlett pears, ripe
  but firm

¼ cup dried cranberries

¼ cup chopped walnuts

½ cup low-fat vanilla Greek
  yogurt

¼ teaspoon ground
  cinnamon

1. Core the pears and chop them into bite-size pieces. Put the chopped pears into a large mixing bowl along with the cranberries and walnuts.

2. Stir in the yogurt and cinnamon until combined. Store in the refrigerator until ready to serve.

INGREDIENT TIP: To ripen pears faster, place them in a bowl at room temperature with other fruit like bananas.

Per Serving: Calories: 196; Fat: 6g; Protein: 3g; Carbohydrates: 38g; Fiber: 6g; Sugar: 26g; Sodium: 22mg

PISTACHIO NICE CREAM

Serves 2 / Prep time: 10 minutes

5 INGREDIENTS OR FEWER, DAIRY-FREE, QUICK, VEGETARIAN

Who knew bananas had an ice cream alter ego? Yes, blending frozen bananas in a food processor transforms them into a creamy frozen treat without added dairy or sugar. Although this version doesn't have the green hue of traditional pistachio ice cream, I promise you won't even realize it's missing when you take the first creamy bite studded with crunchy chopped pistachios.

3 peeled and frozen overripe bananas

½ teaspoon almond extract

½ teaspoon vanilla extract

2 tablespoons unsalted chopped pistachios

1. Slice the frozen bananas into pieces with a sharp knife and put them into a food processor.

2. Add the almond extract and vanilla to the food processor, and blend on high until the mixture is smooth. Scrape down sides as needed.

3. Once the mixture is smooth, stir in the pistachios.

4. Serve immediately for a soft-serve texture, or, for a firmer texture, place the ice cream in a freezer-safe container and freeze for at least 30 minutes.

5. If completely frozen, let it sit on the counter for at least 10 minutes to soften before enjoying.

INGREDIENT TIP: Keep a stockpile of peeled, too-far-gone bananas in your freezer to make this recipe or Creamy Banana Date Shake (page 121) whenever the craving hits.

Per Serving: Calories: 204; Fat: 4g; Protein: 4g; Carbohydrates: 43g; Fiber: 5g; Sugar: 22g; Sodium: 4mg

RASPBERRY MINT SORBET

Serves 2 / Prep time: 8 minutes

5 INGREDIENTS OR FEWER, DAIRY-FREE, QUICK, VEGETARIAN

This refreshing dessert is made from just a handful of healthy ingredients—including raspberries, which are rich in vitamin C—and comes together in less than 10 minutes. Using frozen berries saves money and time. Feel free to adjust the amount of sweetener depending on how much tartness you enjoy.

2 cups frozen raspberries

3 tablespoons water

1 tablespoon honey

1 tablespoon chopped
   fresh mint

1. In a food processor, combine the frozen raspberries, water, honey, and mint, and blend on high until the mixture is smooth, or about 5 minutes. Scrape down the sides of the bowl as needed.

2. If the mixture isn't blending smooth, add an extra tablespoon of water at a time until blended to desired consistency.

3. Serve as is for a soft-serve texture. For a firmer texture, transfer the sorbet to a freezer-safe container and freeze for at least 30 minutes.

4. If enjoying frozen, let it sit on the counter for at least 10 minutes to soften before serving.

SUBSTITUTION TIP: Replace the honey with maple or agave syrup to make this recipe vegan-friendly.

Per Serving: Calories: 106; Fat: 1g; Protein: 2g; Carbohydrates: 26g; Fiber: 9g; Sugar: 15g; Sodium: 5mg

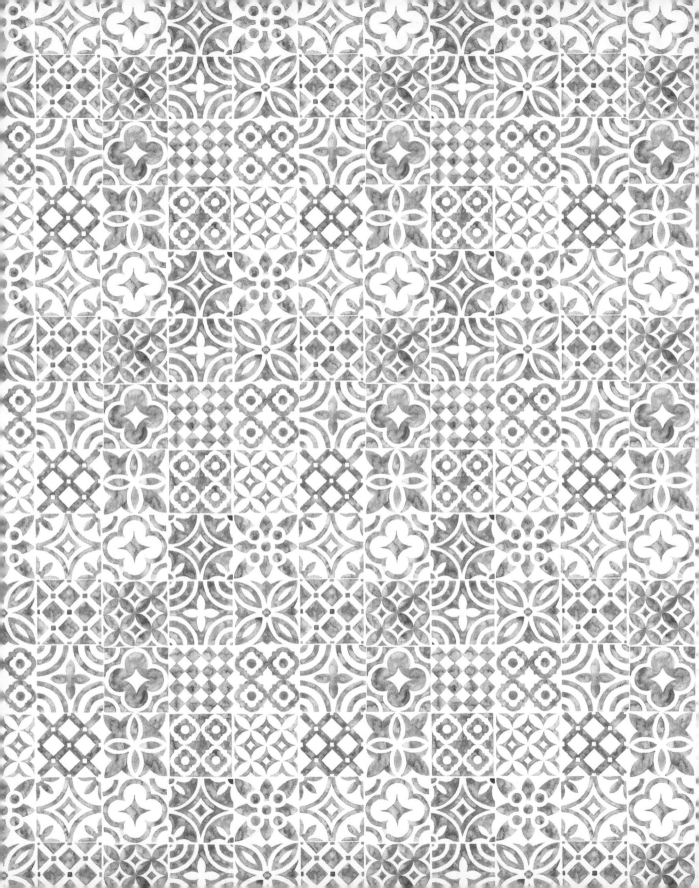

Quick Garlic Hummus, page 134

STAPLES

WALNUT BASIL PESTO

Makes 1 cup / Prep time: 15 minutes

Originating in Genoa, Italy, basil pesto has been enjoyed and modified into many different versions. This back-to-basics recipe swaps out pine nuts for walnuts, which are more readily available and affordable and can be used in many other recipes featured in this book.

2 cups packed chopped
   fresh basil

3 garlic cloves, peeled

¼ cup chopped walnuts

½ cup extra-virgin olive oil

½ teaspoon salt

⅓ cup grated Parmesan
   cheese

1. In a food processor or high-powered blender, combine the basil, garlic, and walnuts. Pulse until the mixture is coarsely chopped.

2. Add the oil, salt, and Parmesan cheese. Process on high for 5 minutes, or until mixture is well mixed and smooth.

3. Refrigerate in a covered container for up to 3 weeks, or store in the freezer for up to 1 month.

VARIATION TIP: Boost the nutrition by replacing ¼ to ½ cup of the basil with baby spinach.

Per Serving (1 tablespoon): Calories: 82; Fat: 9g; Protein: 1g; Carbohydrates: 1g; Fiber: 0g; Sugar: 0g; Sodium: 98mg

QUICK GARLIC HUMMUS

Makes 3 cups / Prep time: 10 minutes

5 INGREDIENTS OR FEWER, DAIRY-FREE, QUICK, VEGETARIAN

Hummus is a quick, easy, and delicious sandwich spread or dip for fresh veggies and whole-grain crackers. Hummus is traditionally made with tahini, a sesame seed spread, tahini can be expensive and sometimes tricky to find. This version skips the tahini, but you'll still get all the nutty creaminess you love, plus all the delicious garlic flavor.

1 (28-ounce) can
   low-sodium chickpeas,
   drained and rinsed

3 garlic cloves, peeled

⅓ cup extra-virgin olive oil

2 tablespoons freshly
   squeezed lemon juice

2 tablespoons water

¼ teaspoon salt

¼ teaspoon ground cumin

1. In a food processor, combine the chickpeas, garlic, oil, lemon juice, water, salt, and cumin. Puree on high until the mixture is smooth, scraping down the sides as needed.

2. Refrigerate for up to 1 week in a covered container.

VARIATION TIP: For a more intense garlic flavor, use 3 to 4 Roasted Garlic cloves (page 135) in place of fresh garlic.

Per Serving (¼ cup hummus): Calories: 107; Fat: 7g; Protein: 3g; Carbohydrates: 9g; Fiber: 2g; Sugar: 2g; Sodium: 129mg

ROASTED GARLIC

Makes 1 bulb / Prep time: 5 minutes / **Cook time:** 40 minutes

5 INGREDIENTS OR FEWER, DAIRY-FREE, VEGETARIAN, WORTH THE WAIT

I could roast garlic for the smell alone, but the intense garlic flavor it lends to anything you add it to is what makes this a staple recipe. It takes a little while to roast, but this is primarily a hands-off recipe, and it can be made ahead of time or along with anything you are already baking in the oven. Add this to mashed potatoes, homemade hummus, and pasta sauce to boost flavor.

1 head garlic

1 teaspoon extra-virgin
   olive oil

Salt

1. Preheat the oven to 400°F. Place a rack in the middle of the oven.

2. Slice off the top quarter of the head of garlic and discard. Wrap the remaining head of garlic in aluminum foil, leaving the top open, and place it in a small, oven-safe ramekin.

3. Drizzle the oil over the top of the garlic and sprinkle it with salt. Wrap the garlic completely with foil.

4. Place the ramekin containing the garlic on the middle rack of the preheated oven. Bake for 40 minutes, or until the garlic cloves are golden and softened.

INGREDIENT TIP: When shopping for garlic, look for unblemished bulbs with dry skins and firm cloves for best quality.

Per Serving: Calories: 93; Fat: 5g; Protein: 2g; Carbohydrates: 12g; Fiber: 1g; Sugar: 0g; Sodium: 161mg

LEMONY GREEK DRESSING

Makes ½ cup / Prep time: 5 minutes

5 INGREDIENTS OR FEWER, DAIRY-FREE, QUICK, VEGETARIAN

The key to turning any salad from drab to fab is all in the dressing. Making your own salad dressings at home is quick and easy and can be a great cost-cutting habit to add to your repertoire. This simple, Greek-inspired dressing is filled with ingredients commonly found in Greek cooking like oregano, garlic, olive oil, and lemon and is great for salads, as a marinade for chicken or pork, or as a dip for chopped vegetables.

¼ **cup extra-virgin olive oil**

¼ **cup freshly squeezed lemon juice**

2 **garlic cloves, minced**

1 **teaspoon dried oregano**

1 **teaspoon Dijon mustard**

½ **teaspoon salt**

¼ **teaspoon freshly ground pepper**

1. In a liquid measuring cup, whisk together the oil, lemon juice, garlic, oregano, mustard, salt, and pepper.

2. Refrigerate in an airtight container for up to 1 week. Let sit at room temperature for 3 minutes, then shake well before using.

SUBSTITUTION TIP: No fresh garlic on hand? Use ½ teaspoon of garlic powder instead.

Per Serving (2 tablespoons): Calories: 126; Fat: 14g; Protein: 0g; Carbohydrates: 2g; Fiber: 0g; Sugar: 0g; Sodium: 305mg

SIMPLE FRENCH VINAIGRETTE

Makes ½ cup / Prep time: 5 minutes

5 INGREDIENTS OR FEWER, DAIRY-FREE, QUICK, VEGETARIAN

This dressing is a variation on my French grandmother's famous recipe, with my own little tweaks. It is one of the simplest dressings, but it is my absolute favorite, because it has the perfect balance of tanginess and sweetness, with extra garlic flavor. If enjoyed from the refrigerator, the oil will be solidified from the cold. Let it sit at room temperature for 5 minutes before using.

¼ cup extra-virgin olive oil

¼ cup white vinegar

2 garlic cloves, minced

½ teaspoon salt

1 teaspoon Dijon mustard

1 teaspoon honey

1. In a liquid measuring cup, whisk the oil, vinegar, garlic, salt, mustard, and honey.

2. Refrigerate in an airtight container for up to 1 week.

VARIATION TIP: Use red wine vinegar or apple cider vinegar in place of the white vinegar to change the flavor profile. Just don't tell my grammy I told you to do it.

Per Serving (2 tablespoons): Calories: 130; Fat: 14g; Protein: 0g; Carbohydrates: 2g; Fiber: 0g; Sugar: 1g; Sodium: 305mg

BALSAMIC GLAZE

Makes ½ cup / Cook time: 20 minutes

5 INGREDIENTS OR FEWER, DAIRY-FREE, QUICK, VEGETARIAN

Balsamic vinegar is a common ingredient in Mediterranean cooking, and heating it into a thick and syrupy glaze takes it to another level. Reducing the vinegar concentrates and intensifies its sweet flavor, making it a great finishing touch on savory and sweet dishes such as grilled chicken, salads, and grilled fruits.

2 cups balsamic vinegar

1. Pour the vinegar into a large saucepan and bring it to a boil over medium heat.

2. Reduce the heat to medium-low and continue simmering, stirring occasionally, for 20 minutes, or until the vinegar is reduced by about half and thickened.

3. Let the glaze cool completely, then refrigerate it in an airtight container for up to 1 week.

SHOPPING TIP: Look for quality vinegar, such as balsamic vinegar of Modena with rich, dark color for best flavor and results. Some of my favorite affordable brands are Colavita or Alessi.

Per Serving (1 tablespoon): Calories: 56; Fat: 0g; Protein: 0g; Carbohydrates: 11g; Fiber: 0g; Sugar: 10g; Sodium: 15mg

BALSAMIC CARAMELIZED ONIONS

Makes 3 cups / Prep time: 5 minutes / **Cook time:** 15 minutes

5 INGREDIENTS OR FEWER, DAIRY-FREE, QUICK, VEGETARIAN

It's no secret that caramelized onions add a lovely flavor to many dishes, but they often take a lot of time and extra oil to cook. This version will give you the same intense flavor, but in a fraction of the time with the extra sweet tang of balsamic vinegar. You'll never make caramelized onions the same way again! These are a great topping on Roasted Red Pepper and Goat Cheese Chickpea Burgers (page 69).

1 tablespoon extra-virgin olive oil

2 large red onions, thinly sliced

Water

¼ teaspoon salt

2 tablespoons balsamic vinegar

1. In a large skillet, heat the oil over medium-high heat. Add the onions and stir to coat them with oil.

2. Cook, stirring often, for 10 to 12 minutes, or until the onions are soft and translucent. Add a tablespoon of water at a time if the onions start to stick.

3. Add the salt and vinegar. Cook for another 1 to 2 minutes, or until the vinegar has evaporated.

SHOPPING TIP: Often, bagged onions are cheaper per pound than buying onions individually. If the bagged onions are smaller, use four small onions instead of the two large onions called for in the recipe.

Per Serving (¼ cup): Calories: 22; Fat: 1g; Protein: 0g; Carbohydrates: 3g; Fiber: 0g; Sugar: 1g; Sodium: 50mg

EASY TZATZIKI

Makes 1 cup / Prep time: 10 minutes

5 INGREDIENTS OR FEWER, QUICK, VEGETARIAN

A popular condiment in Greek cooking, tzatziki (*tsah-zee-kee*) is a cool and creamy sauce that's delicious on gyros, lamb, pitas, and Harissa-Spiced Turkey Burgers with Tzatziki (page 107). Some traditional versions are made with sheep or goat's milk yogurt, but this version is made with plain Greek yogurt, which is readily available at most grocery stores.

½ **English cucumber**

1 cup low-fat plain Greek yogurt

2 garlic cloves, minced

2 tablespoons chopped fresh dill

1½ tablespoons freshly squeezed lemon juice

1 tablespoon extra-virgin olive oil

½ teaspoon salt

1. Using a box grater, grate the cucumber and squeeze out the excess water. Place the cucumber in a large bowl.

2. Add the yogurt, garlic, dill, lemon juice, oil, and salt, and mix well.

3. Cover and refrigerate until ready to serve, or up to 3 days.

INGREDIENT TIP: No fresh dill? No problem! Replace it with 2 teaspoons of dried dill.

Per Serving (2 tablespoons): Calories: 39; Fat: 2g; Protein: 2g; Carbohydrates: 3g; Fiber: 0g; Sugar: 3g; Sodium: 167mg

SUPER-FLUFFY QUINOA

Makes 3 cups / Prep time: 5 minutes / **Cook time:** 25 minutes

5 INGREDIENTS OR FEWER, DAIRY-FREE, QUICK, VEGETARIAN

Quinoa is a nutrient-rich seed that cooks up just like rice or barley, and it is used as an ingredient in many dishes throughout this cookbook. Quinoa is packed with hunger-crushing protein and fiber, and it couldn't be easier to prepare. I'll show you the trick to making this healthy staple superlight and fluffy every time in this recipe.

1 cup quinoa, rinsed

2 cups water

Salt

1. In a large stockpot, combine the rinsed quinoa and water and bring to a boil over medium-high heat.

2. Reduce the heat to medium-low and simmer for 20 minutes, or until all the liquid has been absorbed.

3. Remove the pan from the heat, and cover for 5 minutes. Fluff with a fork and season with salt before serving.

VARIATION TIP: Cook the quinoa in low-sodium vegetable or chicken stock instead of water to enhance the flavor. For a more Mediterranean flavor, cook the quinoa with a bay leaf, 2 peeled garlic cloves, and a couple of sprigs of oregano. Remove the bay leaf, garlic, and oregano sprigs before serving.

Per Serving (1 cup cooked): Calories: 208; Fat: 3g; Protein: 8g; Carbohydrates: 36g; Fiber: 4g; Sugar: 0g; Sodium: 55mg

MEASUREMENT CONVERSIONS

VOLUME EQUIVALENTS	U.S. STANDARD	U.S. STANDARD (OUNCES)	METRIC (APPROXIMATE)
LIQUID	2 tablespoons	1 fl. oz.	30 mL
	¼ cup	2 fl. oz.	60 mL
	½ cup	4 fl. oz.	120 mL
	1 cup	8 fl. oz.	240 mL
	1½ cups	12 fl. oz.	355 mL
	2 cups or 1 pint	16 fl. oz.	475 mL
	4 cups or 1 quart	32 fl. oz.	1 L
	1 gallon	128 fl. oz.	4 L
DRY	⅛ teaspoon	—	0.5 mL
	¼ teaspoon	—	1 mL
	½ teaspoon	—	2 mL
	¾ teaspoon	—	4 mL
	1 teaspoon	—	5 mL
	1 tablespoon	—	15 mL
	¼ cup	—	59 mL
	⅓ cup	—	79 mL
	½ cup	—	118 mL
	⅔ cup	—	156 mL
	¾ cup	—	177 mL
	1 cup	—	235 mL
	2 cups or 1 pint	—	475 mL
	3 cups	—	700 mL
	4 cups or 1 quart	—	1 L
	½ gallon	—	2 L
	1 gallon	—	4 L

OVEN TEMPERATURES

FAHRENHEIT	CELSIUS (APPROXIMATE)
250°F	120°C
300°F	150°C
325°F	165°C
350°F	180°C
375°F	190°C
400°F	200°C
425°F	220°C
450°F	230°C

WEIGHT EQUIVALENTS

U.S. STANDARD	METRIC (APPROXIMATE)
½ ounce	15 g
1 ounce	30 g
2 ounces	60 g
4 ounces	115 g
8 ounces	225 g
12 ounces	340 g
16 ounces or 1 pound	455 g

REFERENCES

Esposito, Katherine, Maria Ida Maiorino, Giuseppe Bellastella, Paolo Chiodini, Demosthenes Panagiotakos, and Dario Giugliano. "A Journey into a Mediterranean Diet and Type 2 Diabetes: A Systematic Review with Meta-analyses." *BMJ Open* 5, no. 8 (August 10, 2015). Accessed November 15, 2021. doi:10.1136 /bmjopen-2015-008222.

Hardman, Roy J., Greg Kennedy, Helen Macpherson, Andrew B. Scholey, and Andrew Pipingas. "Adherence to a Mediterranean-Style Diet and Effects on Cognition in Adults: A Qualitative Evaluation and Systematic Review of Longitudinal and Prospective Trials." *Frontiers in Nutrition* 3 (July 22, 2016). Accessed November 15, 2021. doi:10.3389/fnut.2016.00022.

Martín-Peláez, Sandra, Montse Fito, and Olga Castaner. "Mediterranean Diet Effects on Type 2 Diabetes Prevention, Disease Progression, and Related Mechanisms. A Review." *Nutrients* 12, no. 8 (July 27, 2020): 2236. Accessed November 15, 2021. doi:10.3390/nu12082236.

The National Academies of Science Engineering Medicine. "Report Sets Dietary Intake Levels for Water, Salt, and Potassium To Maintain Health and Reduce Chronic Disease Risk." News release, February 11, 2004. The National Academies. Accessed November 15, 2021. nationalacademies.org/news/2004/02/report -sets-dietary-intake-levels-for-water-salt-and-potassium-to-maintain-health -and-reduce-chronic-disease-risk.

INDEX

ACKNOWLEDGMENTS

I'd first like to thank my unofficial chief tasting officer, husband, and biggest supporter: Rob, thank you for believing that I could write this while also planning our wedding and honeymoon in the same span of time. We did it! Thank you to my parents, who have always let me pave my own road, even if they couldn't see where it led to. It is because of you that I have blossomed into the person I am today. To my friends and family, who are my unofficial PR team, hype crew, and taste testers. For you, I am forever grateful.

ABOUT THE AUTHOR

 **EMILY COOPER**, RD, is an award-winning recipe developer, nationally recognized food and nutrition expert, and registered dietitian born and raised in small-town New Hampshire. She shares quick, easy, and healthy recipes on her website, Sinful Nutrition (SinfulNutrition.com), showcasing that eating and living healthier doesn't have to be boring, difficult, or expensive. She currently resides with her husband in New Jersey.